Praise for The Art of Healthcare Innovation

"Christina eloquently explains complex materials in an accessible way which demonstrates her deeper understanding of the material. Her curiosity is infectious, writing delightful and her work will be beneficial for physicians and patients as well."

—Michael V. Genovese, M.D.,
J.D. Chief Medical Officer, Acadia Healthcare

"This book represents a great achievement. It compiles thoughts of industry leaders on a topic relevant to all of us-healthcare. The insights and perspectives shared here are driving innovation that will impact generations to come"

—Robin Moriarty Ph.D.,
COO, Equifa
Author, What

"A fascinating and insightful book! *The Art of Healthcare Innovation* distills complex concepts into an inspiring, readily-understandable glimpse into the people and ideas that will change our wellbeing for generations to come."

—Marshall Goldsmith,
New York Times #1 Bestselling Author
of *Triggers, Mojo,* and *What Got You Here Won't Get You There*

"From vibrant and passionate Christina D. Warner, author of *The Art of Healthcare Innovation*, comes an enlightening view of how technology and innovative thinking will change healthcare and make a lasting impression on our world for the better! A work of deep learnings and storytelling with the reminder that 'change is the only constant we can count on.' It is an important reality that we must embrace, empowering oneself and those around us, to unlock one's full potential, to being open to the unknown and new ways, and to bring awareness to the importance of taking care of YOU. Healthcare is one of, if not, the biggest issue facing the world today, and advancing this through innovation and awareness is critical. Sincere and revelatory, *The Art of Healthcare Innovation* shares deeply personal experiences and learnings to inspire us to open ourselves up to new thinking and approaches—old ways won't open new learnings."

—Barbara M. Fisher,
Advisor Board Member
Keller Influence Institute™ and Executive

"Christina has assembled a great collection of inspiring and personal stories from important innovators in the field of healthcare today. This book is engaging and accessible, covering a broad range of ideas. Christina has really captured the essence of what motivates these talented individuals and the lessons they have learned along the way."

—Rebecca Mechanik, President,
Pegasus Advisors

"Christina Warmer's book gives us 2 gifts; the solidity of a strong and logic conceptual framework (awareness, diagnosis, treatment, lifestyle change and ongoing care) and the wisdom & creativity of 35 thought leaders and amazing practitioners. A true gem of a book that should be a reference point in Health, the field most disrupted by the 4th Industrial Revolution with the biggest impact on humans in the years to come."

—Paolo Gallo, Best-Selling Author,
Senior Advisor to the World Economic Forum
Executive Chairman

"Good for both quick diversions or longer studies, *The Art of Healthcare Innovation* introduces the people and ideas changing the future of healthcare and organizes them around the patient in a way that is immediately intuitive and actionable."

—Jeffrey Rieske, Senior Manager,
PwC's Health Industries Advisory

"A simple, yet meaningful read that brings everyday healthcare leaders' success and learning closer to all of us inspired to make a difference in the healthcare world."

—Alice Pai,
Business Strategy and Enablement,
CareAllies Inc. (a subsidiary of Cigna).

"I highly recommend *The Art of Healthcare Innovation*. It is an informative, interesting and unique guide to the current leaders of healthcare innovation and healthcare trends. An important read for healthcare enthusiasts, healthcare professionals, thought leaders, and business and management leaders."

—John Corcoran, Co-CEO,
Rise25 and Former White House aide

"Christina D. Warner has compiled a must-read primer for anyone considering a career in healthcare or has an avid interest in the future of work. Read and learn from the experts."

—Dorie Clark, author
of *Reinventing You* and *Stand Out*, and
Executive Education Faculty, Duke University Fuqua
School of Business.

The Art of Healthcare Innovation

Interviews and Industry Insights
from 35 Game-Changing Pioneers

Christina D. Warner

Sheridan & Madison Press

ISBN 978-1-7331496-0-0: E-book
ISBN 978-1-7331496-1-7: Paperback
Library of Congress Control Number: 2019911011
Publisher: Sheridan & Madison Press

For my mother

As a thank you for downloading this book, I would like to give you a supplementary

e-book 100% FREE!

Download
The Quick Guide to Healthcare Innovation

by visiting
www.christinadwarner.com/member

Contents

Letter To The Reader

Dear Reader,

Yes, you! I am very excited to be here, right now, sharing the amazing ideas and wisdom of our present day Einsteins and da Vincis.

Growing up, I was surrounded by heroes. I devoured books on Marie Curie, who discovered radioactivity; jotted down words of wisdom from Florence Nightingale, who revolutionized the nursing industry; and adored the teachings of Sigmund Freud, the father of psychology.

Throughout my career in various industries, I've met modern-day innovators and pioneers. They range from the physicians creating 3D-printed hearts to the entrepreneurs revolutionizing data for better decisions and the patient advocates bravely fighting for a voice and a new way.

In this book, I interview visionaries from all walks of life and explore their big ideas about healthcare, how they will change our world, and what they've learned along the way. But most importantly, what we can learn from them.

In the pages that follow, you will have an amazing opportunity to get a rare glimpse of the future. Each of the big ideas, innovations, and treatments is sorted into the steps of a patient journey.

A patient journey is the points of contact a patient will have with a healthcare system. There are many different variations and frameworks for the patient journey. You'll find the different steps in the patient journey in the following sections:

1. Awareness

2. Diagnosis

3. Treatment

4. Lifestyle Change

5. Ongoing Care

Finally, the last section, "Environment", opens up into all of healthcare. It covers a wide range of topics, from entrepreneurship to venture capitalists, career management, and technology in the workplace.

Although each of the big ideas and lessons learned within a section draws on the theme of that section, each chapter can be read as a standalone. Open the book and read wherever you land or choose a particular innovator that interests you most.

Use each chapter as inspiration—learn what amazing, spectacular, and utterly shocking innovations are ahead of us, and jot down words of wisdom that you can learn from.

Our hope (the contributors and my own) is that you will use this book—part crystal ball, part diary—both as a glimpse of what the future holds and as a collection of inspiring stories.

The pioneers have peeled back the walls and given us a snapshot of what could be, and what will be. Through them, we are shaping the future.

I invite you to join us on the journey.

Christina D. Warner

July, 2019

THE ART OF HEALTHCARE INNOVATION

Awareness

The first step of the patient journey is awareness. The patient self-assesses his or her conditions and symptoms, and makes initial contact with the health system.

"We must have perseverance and above all confidence in ourselves. We must believe that we are gifted for something."

—Marie Curie

A DIAGNOSTIC TOOL FOR DEMENTIA DETECTION

Dr. Sina Habibi

CEO, COGNETIVITY NEUROSCIENCES

Cognetivity Neurosciences was founded in 2013 with a mission to redefine dementia detection. We have developed a sensitive diagnostic tool, which runs on Apple iOS devices. It consists of a five-minute test that uses visual stimuli and artificial intelligence to detect mental health disorders such as dementia, even at very early stages, without the need for a healthcare professional to be present.

After my grandmother was diagnosed with dementia, I did some research into the condition and soon found that there was an enormous global problem. Dementia will affect one in three children born today and cost $500 billion globally every year. The cost of treatment is expected to reach $2 trillion globally by 2030. According to estimates, early diagnosis of the disease has the potential to save $118,000 per patient.

Not only is the number of patients growing, but half of those with dementia in the United States and United

Kingdom never receive a formal diagnosis. And those that are diagnosed often receive their diagnosis so late that their options for treatment and planning are limited. The dementia tests that are used at the moment are crude. In some cases, doctors don't even use pen and paper tests to make referrals. Instead they rely on patients to determine if their memory is good enough. By the time the patient has a problem remembering their children's names, it's almost certainly too late to undertake any meaningful intervention and the problem becomes extremely difficult for patients and expensive for healthcare systems.

Our integrated cognitive assessment (ICA) tool looks for the earliest signs of impairment by testing the performance of large areas of the brain. It can also be used for remote monitoring of the progression of diseases and for measuring the effectiveness of treatments. We believe that the test we've developed is a completely novel platform. By combining visual stimulation techniques developed through cutting-edge neuro-scientific research and artificial intelligence, our ICA test measures something quite different to any other test and can measure cognitive function with a high level of sensitivity. The ICA is particularly suitable for testing large numbers of people. Unlike currently used tests, it doesn't suffer from learning, education, language and culture effects.

Through enabling earlier detection, patient care can be significantly improved through treatment and lifestyle changes. Researchers will also have the opportunity to develop new treatments, being able to assess their effect on patients at earlier stages of cognitive impairment. This represents a major unmet need in the fight against dementia—the biggest healthcare challenge of the twenty-first century.

Q&A WITH SINA HABIBI

What brought you to this career?

Towards the end of my PhD, I became frustrated with the pace of research in academia and found the world of venture creation a lot more inspiring. This observation and drive led me to join Cambridge University Entrepreneurs, a society dedicated to spinning out various ventures from the university. I was chairing the society by the end of my PhD when I met my co-founder, Dr. Seyed-Mahdi Khaligh-Razavi, and started working on Cognetivity.

How did you get funding initially?

Soon after we conceptualized Cognetivity, there was a global startup competition in Cambridge. Over 150 companies had entered the competition, some of which already had a few million dollars in funding. We only entered the competition in order to be able to attend the conference but, to our surprise, we won the competition and this provided our initial funding to start the company.

If you had a million dollars, what would you invest in?

Early disease detection. This area of research furthers our understanding of disease pathways and can lead to new treatments and ultimately to prevention. Technologies that I think will certainly see continued growth over the next couple of years in healthcare are AI, deep learning and data mining.

Follow on Twitter: @Cognetivity

GENOME SEQUENCING FOR PERSONALIZED TREATMENTS

Dennis Grishin

COFOUNDER AND CHIEF SCIENTIFIC OFFICER,
NEBULA GENOMICS AND BOEHRINGER INGELHEIM PHD
FELLOW IN GENETICS AND GENOMICS,
HARVARD UNIVERSITY

Our mission is to drive the adoption of personal genome sequencing and the sharing of genomic data. The availability of large genomic datasets will have a huge impact on healthcare. It will enable researchers to understand why we get sick and how to create personalized treatments.

Today, many people can already benefit greatly from sequencing their genomes. It enables one to understand disease risks and take preventive actions, avoid drugs that are likely to have side effects, and reduce the risk of having children that are affected by severe genetic conditions. The benefits of personal genome sequencing are growing rapidly as researchers learn more about human genetics.

In terms of the potential drawbacks, genetic information could be misused to discriminate and stigmatize people. For example, a person may be denied insurance because of genetically determined risks. Discrimination in other areas such as employment, education, and housing is also conceivable.

Genetics may also affect personal relationships because people who are carriers for genetic diseases, or who have undesirable traits, might encounter difficulty in finding a partner. Such risks deter many people from genetic testing. Nebula Genomics seeks to address this issue by offering a privacy-focused personal genomics service that relies on multiple cryptographic techniques to protect their data.

Q&A WITH DENNIS GRISHIN

What brought you to this career?

In 2015, I started my PhD in genomics in the laboratory of Prof. George Church at Harvard Medical School. I began working on a new DNA sequencing method to determine regions of the human genome that had not been sequenced to date, due to the limitations of our current technology. While working on this project, I realized that already-available and affordable DNA sequencing technology was severely underutilized because it had not been widely adopted by patients and consumers. My co-founders and I started Nebula Genomics to enable affordable personal genome sequencing and give people control over personal genomic data.

What do you believe in?

I have always tried to work on important, difficult problems. While this maximizes the chances of having a significant impact, it also leads to many failures. I found it easier to deal with this by adopting a stoic life philosophy.

What advice would you give others?

I think it's important to be attentive to opportunities that might unexpectedly arise—and be prepared to take them. Practically, this means having broad interests, interacting with people from different professional backgrounds, and building a generalizable skillset that can be applied to different problems.

Follow on Twitter: @DennisGrishin

BLOCKCHAIN FOR TRUSTED RECORDS

Warren Whitlock

BLOCKCHAIN INFLUENCER AND DIRECTOR, COINAGENDA

Blockchain is the next big thing that will be built on the internet of trust. Blockchain uses smart contracts, it's interconnected, and it's a permanent type of database. The internet of things and blockchain will disrupt how we collect data today, and how the data is protected. The data is recorded, it may be encrypted so that only those with permission can access it, and it is permanent and saved in a thousand places.

This is going to fundamentally change how we do things, and how we trust each other. Paperwork and pre-approvals will be simplified and stored in blockchain. Blockchain is also the technology that underpins cryptocurrency, and this could be the way we pay our doctors in the future. For example, our Fitbits will earn us tokens, and when we see a doctor, the doctor will take the tokens as payments.

Finally, there's 5G internet. This is the next generation of internet connection, which will fundamentally impact healthcare by providing the infrastructure necessary to carry large amounts of data. It has the potential to enhance device connectivity, provide higher system capacity, reduce latency and cost. It will expand tele-medicine and its reach, making it more popular. Plus, it can transmit large amounts of imaging and patient data, expand real-time remote monitoring, and support the foundation for AI and blockchain.

Q&A WITH WARREN WHITLOCK

What brought you to this career?

I was trained in business, and business teaches you that it's a dog-eat-dog world. I never really liked this, and I didn't think this was all there was in life. Then I heard about a guy named Zig Ziglar. I saw him speak and read his books. Right before he died, I was able to be on stage with him and speak at the same event. Zig Ziglar's philosophy is that you can get anything you want out of life if you help enough people get what they want.

As a salesman, I found that I could do so much better by helping people buy instead of trying to sell them something. I became a sales manager and then started my own company. Then the internet came along. I studied advertising and marketing, and sent out email newsletters at a time when most people didn't have email. By the time everyone had email, I was pretty good at this! Then social media came along. I was an early adopter and wrote the book *Twitter Revolution*.

Then bitcoin came out and I learned about bitcoin mining machines, and now I'm an influencer in block-chain. Looking back, I see two common themes. The first is to always give and help others. The second is to be an early adopter of technology.

What advice would you give others?

1. You always get a choice. If someone slapped me in the face, what should my response be? I don't have to slap them back. You decide what is best and knowing that you get to make that decision is critical.

2. There is a quote I often share: "You never know what battles people are struggling with." Most people do not have bad intentions towards you. They are too busy worrying about themselves to care about you.

3. Read the book *Think and Grow Rich*. In the book, the first step is to be definite about what you want. The second step is to figure out what you are willing to sacrifice. The third step is to set a plan. The fourth step is implementing that plan and keeping the plan in mind.

4. It's impossible to go back and live in the past. You have to be in the now, and accept what is going on. If you have a negative emotion, be open, experience it, and then get over it.

Follow on Twitter: @WarrenWhitlock

TELEMEDICINE FOR DENTAL CARE

Dr. Hitesh Tolani

CEO AND FOUNDER, VIRTUDENT

As nations become more interconnected, so does the health and wellbeing of the world's population. We can no longer just look at population health locally or nationally. Instead, we must think of population health as a global partnership that is implemented on the local level. So, how will the best doctors in the world be empowered to help individuals well beyond their borders?

At Virtudent, we believe this occurs through a combination of (1) mid-level providers, (2) new medical devices, and (3) telehealth technologies. We've decided to start with dentistry, a highly tactile and in-person healthcare vertical that 40 percent of the US population can't access and which costs more to treat than all cancer treatments combined. We equip registered dental hygienists with new devices that allow them to provide high-quality preventative care to patients in the field. We use telehealth technologies to connect the hygienists with world-class dentists for supervision, evaluation and diagnosis. Then we work to refer patients to local dentists who can address any recommended follow-up care.

Convenience is one of the primary reasons people skip their recommended dental visits. Missing preventative dental care can lead to tooth decay and loss, gum disease, and a number of serious health concerns including heart disease, diabetes, and even Alzheimer's disease. By partnering with companies like Microsoft, Wayfair, EF Education First and many others, we are making it easy for busy employees to finally make it to the dentist. We take a portion of those profits to make care accessible to 5,000 children for free, many of whom have never been to the dentist in their lives.

In the United States, 164 million work hours are lost due to unplanned dental visits and 45 percent of those with dental insurance don't use their preventative care benefits. We are here to change this. Through our model, we've reduced the cost of basic dental care by one-third. We've brought the most specialized dentists in the country, coupled with high-quality care, to the most underserved and remote populations—improving the quality of life of thousands of patients.

I believe the combination of new medical devices and telehealth technologies will help us bring care to the most remote locations around the globe. This will allow people to stay healthy wherever they live, equalizing healthcare disparities. And if this can be done in dentistry, it can also be done in a number of other healthcare specialties.

Q&A WITH HITESH TOLANI

What brought you to this career?

My parents emigrated to the United States when I was a one-year-old. My father, an entrepreneur on a business visa, ran a chain of clothing stores. But he passed away when I was 13 years old and my mom and I became illegal aliens because his visa was our legal link. Pursuing a resolution led to a national immigration battle, resulting in a private relief bill in the US Congress introduced by Strom Thurmond. Thirty-five thousand Americans wrote their congressional representatives for me and my mom and the case was also fought in the US appellate court system.

Towards the end of this saga, I was fortunate to meet a man who served as a judge in the appellate court system and was favorable towards our case. I asked him, "Is there anything I can do to thank you?" He said, "You want to be a dentist? One day someone will come into your chair who will not be able to afford care. The day you treat that person for free, know that I and everyone who campaigned for you has been thanked!" Those words have echoed in my ears ever since. I will never meet all 35,000 people who wrote or worked behind the scenes to push through our bill. Therefore, treating just one patient pro bono doesn't feel like enough, especially since there is no dearth of patients in the US healthcare system who are in need of care.

Was there a tipping point?

Not long after starting Virtudent, someone who was revered in the world of dentistry told me I was as crazy as Willy Wonka! "Your idea to use telemedicine for dentistry is pure imagination," he told me. "If you see even one patient, I'll send you a bottle of Dom Perignon!" He then laughed at me in a room full of people, many of whom were considered titans of dentistry. They all laughed along and I remember walking out of that room feeling quite deflated. But I thought, why not me? I can do this! Today, we treat thousands of patients at Virtudent and I have also gained a mentor—someone revered in the world of dentistry—who has made me the proud owner of a very expensive bottle of Dom. It sits in my office reminding me that good things come to those who hustle!

What have you learned?

1. The 80/20 rule. As a doctor, I am a perfectionist when it comes to treating my patients. However, as a business leader, it is sometimes important to launch products or ideas before achieving perfection.

2. Bite your tongue, whether or not you're right, however asinine the other person is to you. You'll never regret walking away.

3. Your team comes first! It's not your team's job to adapt to you, it's your job to adapt to them. You are as strong as the team you surround yourself with. They will be the reason you succeed, but they won't be the reason you fail.

4. Say thank you! Being grateful is a state of living. It's not a moment in time that's dismissed after two words. It's the way you carry yourself, interact with people, and treat those who challenge you. Sincerely thanking people brings them joy and being grateful pays back in droves.

5. It never gets easy! Building a business is hard work. No matter how big you get or how much money you've raised, there will always be a challenge to solve. If you ever get comfortable, you should be worried.

Follow on Twitter: @DocTolani

LANGUAGE SOLUTIONS FOR NON-ENGLISH SPEAKERS

Scott W. Klein

CEO, LANGUAGELINE SOLUTIONS

One in five of our neighbors here in the United States speak a language other than English at home. One in nine is considered limited English proficient, meaning they are entitled to language assistance by law when seeking healthcare. A million residents are considered "functionally deaf," while 10 million are hard of hearing. Without language access, all of these people are on unequal footing when it comes to addressing their health needs. This is one key pain point. When done right, language access restores their equal footing. It positively affects health outcomes, increases patient satisfaction, elevates staff productivity, and manages costs.

LanguageLine Solutions has been the leader in innovative language-access solutions since 1982. The company sets the global standard for phone, video, and on-site interpreting, as well as translation, localization, and testing and training for bilingual staff and interpreters. LanguageLine is trusted by more than 28,000 clients to enable communication with the limited English proficient, deaf, and hard-of-hearing communities. LanguageLine provides the industry's fastest and most dependable access to more than 9,000 professional linguists in more than 240 languages—24 hours a day, seven days a week, 365 days a year.

We founded the over-the-phone interpreting industry in 1982, and now we work with 13 of America's top 14 medical facilities. Today, we're the largest provider in the language-access industry, with well over 10,000 highly trained, highly skilled linguists. Listing these numbers may sound haughty, but this is an industry where size truly does matter. That's because we are able to immediately scale to our clients' needs, no matter how unanticipated those needs may be. Recently, we handled over 100,000 Spanish interpretation calls in a single day. Those calls were answered in an average of six seconds, as compared to an industry standard of 30 seconds.

Our strategy is to be able to deliver whatever language solution our clients need. We have over-the-phone interpretation, which gives our clients access to over 240 spoken languages. We can also provide video interpretation in 34 spoken languages, plus American and British sign language. And on top of that, we can deliver an on-site interpreter for just about any language that's spoken in the United States. We couple that with a full suite of translation and localization services for the written word, as well as our testing and training solutions.

We also work with healthcare providers to make sure the proper modality is being used at the appropriate time. For example, you don't need an on-site interpreter to help someone register at a hospital. That can easily be done over the phone. You don't need an on-site interpreter at triage or at the point of service delivery. However, if you have some bad news for a family about a loved one that might be very ill, a phone or video solution might not be appropriate. Having one of our interpreters right there in the room might be better. Whatever the need, we have the proper modality to solve the problem in the fastest, most cost-effective way.

Here's the other pain point we address. Typically, when we start to engage with a new client, they quickly figure out that they can get all of their language needs taken care of by using just one company. They can stop doing business with — in some cases — dozens of other providers. This creates tremendous efficiency for them.

There's no more important venue for what we do than healthcare. What I always think about is what it would be like for me if I was traveling with my wife in a foreign country. What if something happened to one of us and we had to go to a hospital where no one spoke English. It would be disorienting and terrifying. I would feel powerless. Empathy is what fuels our business and I always keep that in mind.

Q&A WITH SCOTT W. KLEIN

What brought you to this career?

I've worked in a lot of different industries and for a lot of different businesses. When I worked for Pepsi, it made me crazy if anyone drank anything other than Pepsi. At the end of the day, though, nobody died as a result of their soft drink decision. But at LanguageLine, if we don't do what we do well, people can potentially lose their lives. I was attracted to the fact that all of LanguageLine's team members have a much higher sense of purpose than anywhere else I've ever been.

What difference does language make in healthcare?

When we first launched video interpreting, a hospital was using it for a very sensitive procedure with a non-English speaker. The patient couldn't move. He was awake, all this activity was going on around him, and he couldn't speak English. Yet he was able to make eye-to-eye contact with the interpreter and be kept in the loop with what was going on. It was really something special. Shortly after joining the company, I found out just how important our solutions were to healthcare clients' success or failure. Their desire to work with us to continually enhance the patient experience was unusually collaborative. It's not a buyer-seller relationship. It revolves around collaboration and joint implementation to get the best result for the patient.

What have you learned?

At the beginning of my career, I frequently mistook activity for progress. I wish I had understood earlier how to focus on the most important things, rather than gravitating toward those things that were easy to accomplish. I wish I had known earlier the importance of process and process improvement. That was a huge step change for me when I started going through Six Sigma training 30 years ago. During my first week, it was as if someone had turned the lights on in a dark room. I began to look at everything differently as a result.

Follow on Twitter: @LanguageLine

Diagnosis

The second step of the patient journey is diagnosis. The patient is assessed at the hospital through a variety of tests.

"I'm fascinated by the idea that genetics is digital. A gene is a long sequence of coded letters, like computer information. Modern biology is becoming very much a branch of information technology."

—Richard Dawkins

NEXT-GENERATION DIAGNOSTICS: "OPEN-ACCESS" INSTRUMENTS FOR RAPID DETECTION OF PATHOGENS

Dr. Jack Regan

CEO AND FOUNDER, LEXAGENE

Influenza is one of the deadliest pathogens of all time. The 1918 Spanish flu pandemic killed between 20 and 50 million people in 18 months. Despite 100 years of preparation, we are not much better off today. The world's population has quadrupled, world travel is common, and our front-line healthcare providers only have diagnostics that cannot be quickly configured to detect a new pathogen that may cause the next pandemic. In other words they are non-configurable or "closed-access". Due to this deficiency, our healthcare system is currently not strong enough to respond well to a pandemic, as emergency rooms and medical clinics would be overrun and our ability to provide quality care would drop significantly.

Closed-access instruments are pre-configured with diagnostic tests to screen for a defined set of pathogens. The identity of the targeted pathogens cannot be changed without months of work at R&D and manufacturing facilities, since the reagents for detecting the pathogens are embedded deep inside very complex microfluidic cartridges used by the instrument. The cartridges used by these instruments cannot be quickly configured to detect a new threat. This means that healthcare providers using the technology will get only negative results when these instruments process samples from patients infected with the new pathogen.

Not being able to properly identify the cause of the infection leaves healthcare providers blind to the threat. Since a negative result cannot be used to justify placing a patient in quarantine, the lack of a proper diagnosis gives the new pathogen time to infect others, making a pandemic more likely. To address this problem, healthcare providers need automated pathogen detection instruments at the point-of-care that can be easily configured to detect new strains. In other words, they need "open-access" instruments so that they can more quickly respond to the next pathogen that is capable of causing the next pandemic.

By adopting easy-to-use, open-access pathogen detection instruments, healthcare providers have the ability to customize the instrument to detect new threats. This is important, since the biological world we live in is constantly changing. For example, the CDC (Centers for Disease Control and Prevention) recently reported that nine new pathogens emerged during a 13-year span in the United States. Currently, when new threats arise that cannot be detected by the closed-access instruments on the market, the patient samples must be shipped to a reference laboratory for testing, which takes days to return results.

The beauty of automated open-access pathogen detection instruments placed at the point-of care is that they perform the complex work of a reference laboratory and are capable of returning results in just one hour, allowing for quick, decisive action. Equipping hospitals with open-access instruments gives the healthcare providers a powerful pandemic prevention tool, as they will better be able to triage patients, placing only those infected with the deadly strain into quarantine.

Ordering pathogen-specific tests that can be used by open-access instruments is relatively easy. It's very much like ordering a book from your local library and having it delivered to your doorstep. LexaGene's goal is to make this process as easy as possible. To advance our diagnostics so that the world is better prepared for the next deadly pathogen, investment needs to be made in technologies that can be placed in near-patient settings, such as hospital emergency rooms and medical clinics. To meet this need, LexaGene is working on commercializing the first ever, easy-to-use, open-access instrument. Widespread adoption of LexaGene's technology will enable front-line healthcare providers to better manage the care of their patients, prevent illnesses from spreading, and lowering the cost of care.

Q&A WITH JACK REGAN

How did you get involved in pathogen detection?

I spent my doctoral work creating recombinant (i.e. mutant) influenza viruses. My post-doctoral work focused on developing automated instruments to better detect respiratory pathogens, including influenza and related viruses, and even weaponized anthrax, smallpox, and plague. After completing the development of the first generation of these microfluidic instruments, the natural progression was to further improve these automated bio-detectors so that they could be successfully used in multiple different markets.

Why did the Department of Homeland Security adopt technology you helped to develop?

I joined Lawrence Livermore after UCSF, where I honed my ability to genetically engineer the influenza virus. At first, it wasn't clear exactly what I'd be doing there. I was informed that there would be a vigorous background check, which involved interviewing past professors, neighbors, friends, and even my high-school science teacher. I started wondering whether the government was going to ask me to reverse-engineer the 1918 influenza pandemic strain for the purpose of biological warfare. To my relief, the request was to help develop autonomous surveillance systems to detect biological attacks by rogue nations.

What else are you working on besides pathogen defense?

Our technology is intended to be used by healthcare providers to enable them to more rapidly diagnose their patients and choose the appropriate therapy for better outcomes. We expect our technology to also be used to prevent illnesses from occurring by improving our ability to detect contaminated food items (i.e. food safety). The centralization of food processing plants has had the unintended consequence of making outbreaks more damaging. The food industry needs advanced genetic analyzers, like LexaGene's, that will offer very rapid and very sensitive risk assessment of food items so food producers and packagers can provide safer food and beverage items to their customers.

How can we improve the healthcare system?

The cost of healthcare in the United States is exploding without a commensurate improvement in the quality of care. Although maligned by many, single-payer systems can better manage costs, if done properly. Less money goes toward the overhead associated with insurance companies and more toward providing care. We also need to increase our access to healthcare such that appointments with specialists can be made in days rather than weeks or months, which is the norm. This could be achieved by increasing enrollment at medical schools or opening new medical schools.

Follow on Twitter: @lexa_gene

Dr. Jean P. Gelinas

CEO, XERUS MEDICAL

Medical care is in the early stages of being transformed by the same IT forces that are disrupting so much of the human experience. In some ways, healthcare is trying to catch up to the consumer market. Leveraging medical data to improve care and make it more efficient is seen as being one of the next big innovations and commercial opportunities. Consumer and medical data are also starting to intersect and merge. Giant IT companies now routinely know more about patients than the doctors directly caring for them.

Xerus Medical was founded to gather and analyze the type of patient-centric data that enables humans and machines to synergistically improve care. We automatically analyze the myriad streams of sensor data, from both consumer and purpose-built medical sensors. We integrate the data with electronic medical records and present the information in a meaningful way for clinicians and patients so that their decisions result in better patient outcomes. As we started working on this project, we noticed that the type of data that experienced clinicians and "trained" computers thrive upon overlap but are often very different and complementary.

We strongly believe that wise collection and analysis of various "uncorrelated", but patient-centric, data streams will revolutionize how and where healthcare workers and patients interact and the therapeutic options they choose. The data we collect and analyze enables clinicians to better understand how post-surgical pain, nausea, sleep disturbances and mobility interact and are often codependent. Patients experiencing significant postoperative pain, nausea and anxiety tend to move less and recuperate more slowly. Pain and nausea treatments can potentially over-sedate patients and also decrease mobility and recovery.

The effects of sleep disruption on perioperative [post-surgical] recovery are meaningfully underestimated. That's partly because we do not routinely measure sleep quality in the perioperative context and do not consider it when trying to understand the post-surgical patient experience. By striving to understand the patient's surgical experience in a holistic manner, we believe we can meaningfully improve not only postoperative pain, nausea, mobility, and quality of sleep but also speed up postoperative recovery and decrease appropriate discharge times.

I experienced the lack of quality feedback at first hand when I worked as an anesthesiologist at a daycare surgery center. As I was leaving one day, a nurse told me she was impressed that my patients generally did not have much nausea postoperatively. I felt proud! But the next week, at a same-day surgery center, another nurse said that I should try and minimize my patient's postoperative nausea. I had changed nothing in my medical practice in that brief time interval.

From then on, I started giving out more anti-nausea prophylaxis and asked the nurses more frequently how my patients were doing. The answers seemed almost random and most days, my patients ended up with so many different post-anesthetic care nurses that it was impossible for me to obtain a realistic evaluation. It was clear that the basic quality of feedback needed to become widespread to meaningfully and reproducibly improve care.

Of course, we don't have to gaze into the distant future to see the potential pitfalls of individuals collecting and sharing personal data with commercial service providers. The question is: when does data from wearable devices stop being just for consumer fitness and instead become a medically useful diagnostic tool? Healthcare service providers have some of the most stringent privacy standards, but social networks and search engine companies handle private data in very uneven ways. Internet service providers are tightly regulated, and some consumer wearable companies like Apple are fairly stringent with their privacy rules, but others may not be.

Moreover, some insurance companies now routinely "request" various levels of access to personal data. What might happen if the government or insurance companies insisted, with or without individual consent, on having access to data from consumer devices? Might patients then be denied certain types of care unless they take at least 5,000 steps a day for the next month, for example? Might insurance companies insist you get up from your desk and walk at least once an hour to keep your premiums from going up? And could your employer ask how many hours you slept or analyze your walking patterns to find out if you were under the influence of alcohol or drugs?

In the past, one of the barriers to innovation in healthcare was the length of time it took to get feedback. Clinicians need feedback to be assured that new therapies were performing as well as anticipated, and didn't have unforeseen negative consequences. It took the medical system almost 20 years to gather the necessary data to show that most patients weren't benefiting, or were harmed, by Pulmonary Artery Catheter (PAC) monitoring technology. But now, because of the way data is currently collected and managed, we could potentially reach these types of important conclusions in a fraction of the time.

Modern data management and analysis will radically improve the way we design and perform many types of clinical trials. Quality improvement will become deeply integrated with medical care, and we will look back and be amazed that it was not always so.

Q&A WITH JEAN P. GELINAS

What brought you to this career?

As a young physician, critical care fascinated me. Critical care doctors have to make quick and critical clinical decisions based on information that's often very incomplete. They have access to an enormous amount of data and have to rapidly triage this to make the best decisions for a patient. As a junior physician, I often found it difficult to make sense of so much information quickly. With time and experience, the data became less intimidating and I started wanting access to more. I think this happens because clinical experience creates a sort of pattern-recognition expertise. Computers are extremely good at pattern recognition and I (and many others) thought that "putting the clinical experience in a box" would be highly desirable for patients and society at large.

When did you come to realize the importance of feedback?

As a clinician, there was no way for me to obtain objective feedback about how my patients evolved when they were no longer in my care. Siloed care makes it easy to lose track of our patients. It's usually possible to access feedback on very negative outcomes. But more subtle outcomes, especially over a long period, are more difficult or even impossible to obtain. It's hard for a clinician, computer or any larger system to systematically improve granular care without having comprehensive and well-organized longitudinal feedback.

When I was a young intensivist, I became an expert in the analysis of data derived from an invasive monitoring tool called the Pulmonary Artery Catheter (PAC). Over the years, I and other clinicians suspected that PACs seemed to cause significant mechanical and infectious complications and started to question their use. Eventually, trials showed no benefit (or even harm) in patients who were routinely monitored using PACs. But most clinicians wouldn't change their practice. Over time, the routine use of PACs declined slowly and then abruptly stopped. I think physicians would have transitioned away from this invasive technology a lot faster if they could have seen that outcomes weren't negatively affected. I also learned that advocating against something that's part of your professional claim to fame is not a good career move.

What do you believe in?

Question everything, read avidly and widely, learn, and don't take conventional wisdom as being the truth. At the same time, keep in mind that no matter how knowledgeable, informed and good you become, if you aren't a nice person to work with, things will be much harder than they have to be.

DATA ANALYTICS FOR SOCIAL AND HEALTH SERVICES

Dr. Alina Turner

CEO AND CO-FOUNDER, HELPSEEKER

HelpSeeker curates information on social and health services across jurisdictions, and on how those seeking services are interacting with them. For the first time in Canada, we will have a national dataset on social and health needs and assets at our fingertips. The power of this is immense: we are already merging datasets to run new regressions and find connections between the types of services in a community, how people access these in real-time, and other macro indicators. For instance, we have developed a predictive model for suicide rates and homelessness. We plan on pushing this analysis further by analyzing the sources of funding for health and social services, their distribution per capita, and the impact on population health.

The country is spending a lot, but are we spending enough on the right stuff? That is a question I still can't answer. We have generated financial analysis on service spending to better understand the sources of revenues and where it's going. Over half a trillion dollars are invested in Canada's social safety net annually through non-profits and charities. Is this enough? Clearly not, but is this because the rest of the social safety net doesn't prevent people from becoming homeless? In one city, they were spending $150,000 per person on homelessness services. That amount of money would pay for a home and personal staff for each person and still have some left over. Clearly, we need to take a deeper look at how we came to the current model and see if a better way is possible. Universal basic income might be something worth exploring.

Beyond the implications of HelpSeeker's work for public policy and the way we invest in NGOs and government services, our platform is turning data into analytics to support better decision-making for funders, philanthropists, and service providers. We are also making the dataset available for free to anyone needing help online and via native apps. This democratizes and demystifies the helping sector in a way that consumers can better navigate.

Using the user-behavior data, we are now able to develop our AI component to provide better help-resource suggestions, wading through more than 100,000 listings in Canada alone for the best fit for a client's needs. The ability of clients to provide feedback will create continuous improvement of services, bringing standard practice in the service sector to the fingertips of vulnerable populations.

I am doing a lot thinking right now about the readiness of the sector in light of advancements in machine learning and automation. I am optimistic that we will figure it out but I think human services will be among the last to consider how to prepare for these changes. There is a sense that we are immune because we deal with humans. Yet I am witnessing considerable shifts that would indicate that we too will see mass transformations ahead.

Q&A WITH ALINA TURNER

Where did you grow up?

I was born and raised in Romania during communism, and emigrated to Canada via Germany after 1989. As a kid, I watched the execution of [Romanian president] Nicolae Ceausescu. One day we sang hymns to the man in school and the next we cheered the gunshots. This showed me early on that social systems are a construct —the same way you build them up, you can dismantle them—for good or evil. That set me up for a career studying cultures and social movements.

I lived in poverty for my entire childhood. When I came to Canada as a refugee, I experienced some of the same challenges newcomers are still struggling with today. Comparing my life to my little brother's, I can't help but try to discern what set our paths apart to such an extent. We come from the same family and background but he struggled with mental health, addictions, and involvement in crime from an early age—he never formally finished grade 7. I want better for him, so what can I control or influence to raise that bar?

What brought you to this career?

I studied cultural anthropology with a focus on social movements as a grad student in Canada, then moved into the NGO sector. After that, I bounced between academia and policy advocacy work. I became increasingly disillusioned with the charity model, which is foundational to much of our efforts to address homelessness, poverty, and health disparities. This eventually brought me to the combination of tech innovation, social science research, and practical systems transformation work. I run a consulting firm (Turner Strategies) and a SaaS B-Corp (HelpSeeker), and hold an academic appointment as fellow at the School of Public Policy at the University of Calgary.

What has surprised you most in your work?

Sometimes our sector doesn't want feedback. I realized soon after launching HelpSeeker that the "customer is king" approach was not necessarily the case for NGOs and governments services. In fact, our approach to allow for client feedback per program was met with resistance. Some organizations said their clients couldn't "handle" giving meaningful input, or that the feedback would cause them to lose funding. It was surprising to have this bubble burst for me, though we kept on with the feedback component nonetheless.

I was also shocked at just how overwhelming it was to navigate NGO and government services. It took us over a year of data mining, curating, and cleaning to make sense of about 100,000 services in Canada alone, each with their target groups, eligibility criteria, program models, and referral processes. It's no wonder that people can't find the help they need.

Follow on Twitter: @HelpSeekerOrg

SINGLE-CELL DNA ANALYSIS TO TREAT CANCER

Charlie Silver

CEO AND CO-FOUNDER, MISSION BIO

We think of DNA as the key to life, but it's actually just the molecule that drives cell function. Cancer is fundamentally a single-cell disease—of the 37 trillion cells in the human body, it takes just one cancerous cell to drive the disease forward. The good news is that new targeted therapies have been approved to treat leukemia—but drug resistance and disease progression remain a challenge.

Cancer evolves within the patient in response to treatment, and often away from treatment, leading to disease progression or relapse. Current methods in cancer care include traditional bulk next-generation sequencing (NGS), which relies on sample averages and therefore misses the underlying genetic diversity driving the disease and impacting treatment response.

To effectively combat cancer—to both detect it sooner and develop the most impactful, dynamic therapies—we need to be able to understand it. This means tracking the progression of each and every cancerous cell. At Mission Bio, we're tackling this problem by giving researchers and clinicians the precision and resolution to look at disease origins and paths of progression.

Our first-of-its-kind single-cell DNA analysis technology, the Tapestri® Platform, tracks every cell and every mutation, empowering researchers and clinicians to better predict and prevent cancer relapse. So far, our technology has been used by leading cancer research centers like MD Anderson Cancer Center, University of California San Francisco (UCSF), University of Pennsylvania (Penn), and Stanford University. The technology has also been adopted by leading biopharma companies to help them accelerate their drug development pipelines.

Dr. Koichi Takahashi of the MD Anderson Cancer Center has conducted the largest research study ever done in single-cell using Tapestri. Involving 70 patients, it's the first study of its kind to fully characterize the landscape of subclones in acute myeloid leukemia (AML) tumors and reveal a heterogeneity link to cancer relapse. Most recently, Tapestri's unique sensitivity empowered researchers at UCSF and Penn to monitor the evolution of AML in response to targeted therapy, ultimately revealing how specific mutations drove subsequent therapy resistance in patients. The study, published in *Cancer Discovery*, ultimately uncovered the potential for more impactful, dynamic therapy development and application for those with the disease.

Precision medicine promises better insight into disease and personalized treatments. But so far it has failed to deliver on this promise—largely because we lack the level of insight required to make an impact. In monitoring clinical resistance at the single-cell level, we have the potential to develop therapies that mirror the dynamism of cancer. In short, these findings put us on the precipice of the next frontier of precision medicine. Empowering breakthroughs that can save patient lives is key to our work at Mission Bio. Our Tapestri Platform is uniquely equipped to translate meaningful discoveries in single-cell genomics to the clinic, where a real difference can be made in patient care and ultimate outcomes.

Our technology is not only capable of accurately measuring underlying genetic diversity in blood cancers and solid tumors, but it also serves as a quality control method for CRISPR. While CRISPR holds enormous potential for medical advances, innovation has been hindered by the inability to see the effects of treatment at the single-cell level and to document potential risks.

With Tapestri's single-cell technology, researchers are able to detect both on-target and off-target effects in each and every cell, providing an unprecedented level of insight into the consequences of gene-editing experiments. In fact, as a member of the National Institute of Standards and Technology (NIST) Genome Editing Consortium, Mission Bio now stands as the only single-cell DNA analysis platform providing quality control for CRISPR gene editing.

One of our first customers at Mission Bio was a doctor researcher at Memorial Sloan Kettering Cancer Center. He survived leukemia and now treats AML patients, running research studies to help identify better treatments. In 2018, he presented the results of his research using Mission Bio's technology at a cancer research conference. He told me he'd adopted the technology because he believes he can use it to cure his patients. This story shaped my thinking about what we do at Mission Bio—it's about making the best impact and enabling others to have an impact in the work that drives them.

Q&A WITH CHARLIE SILVER

What brought you to this career?

I've always been interested in building technologies that enable us to understand how the world works, and how we can make it work better. In college, I studied experimental astrophysics and worked in a lab that developed hardware for next-generation telescopes. I took time off from graduate school to work at NASA, where I developed technology for sensitive detectors, which were later used in telescopes designed to see to the edge of the universe and the beginning of time. At my previous company, I developed a new type of electron microscope for imaging the surfaces of materials and biological samples, to elucidate basic biology and materials science.

While physics can offer a deeper appreciation of the world around us, I've come to appreciate how the latest in physics and science can offer insights into the world within us. When I spun Mission Bio out of UCSF, I endeavored to build a technology that would enable better understanding of disease and thereby open up more durable treatments for patients. At Mission Bio, we turn our telescopes inward to view the building blocks of life—DNA—within every cell that harbors disease. By analyzing disease-causing biology with the resolution and scale required to appreciate the full biological system, we enable researchers and clinicians to study and treat disease at its most basic level.

What have you learned in running your business?

We learned over time that market validation is the number one proof point that investors need before they will help us scale. We started the company through a large contract with J&J to support their work in identifying circulating tumor cells. When we pivoted into clinical applications for single-cell genomics, we ran pharma and academic pilot studies to validate the technology and market fit. We also ran a robust beta program on the product to convince ourselves that we were ready to scale our technology. If we had entered the market without this validation behind us, we would have over-engineered the product, and might have missed the window for the market opportunity.

What's important when it comes to hiring people?

When you're scaling up a start-up, by definition no one has ever built this product before. The best you can do is hire for adjacent skill sets, with the agility and breadth of experience to support you wherever the technology and market might go. Our technology development really took off when we hired a top head of R&D who had developed similar products at public and VC-backed companies. That level of experience in the early days was invaluable, and we would have spent much longer developing the product if we hadn't brought in the experience right from the beginning.

It's important to bring in top expertise to your board of directors and advisory as early as possible. There was a breakpoint in our trajectory after we recruited top talent onto our board. The combination of deep domain expertise, commercial background, and start-up building experience gave everyone comfort that our leadership team will nurture and support us on our path to growth. By landing on world-class investors and board members, we brought credibility to investors, customers, and employees.

How do you approach IP?

Other players in our space have aggressively stepped on other IP in their efforts to move quickly, resulting in lawsuits once they started to scale. We took great measures from the beginning to shore up our IP and steer clear of adjacent technologies, and our thoughtful approach built credibility with investors.

How do you approach investors?

We lined up with angel and VC investors who required a financial return but also shared our vision of enabling precision medicine for better patient care. There have been times over the years when different perspectives on tactics emerged. But our shared vision to help sick people kept us anchored so the strategy followed suit.

What do you believe in?

I surround myself with the best and brightest people in every discipline. Within my closest circle are those who share my drive and vision—employees, board, investors, advisors, network. I hire and work with people who are role models to me. I've built a structure and cadence into my life that prioritizes the most important people. I carve out time every day to have breakfast and dinner with my family, and I try to join my son for bedtime whenever I'm within 100 miles of home. And I walk my dog every day.

What advice would you give others?

It's all about focus and saying no. Constantly identify the one or two activities that can have the biggest impact over the next year. Focus on nothing but these, and say no to everything else. Identify the best people who can execute pieces of the vision, then incentivize and motivate them. Trust them with the vision and get out of their way, so you can focus on the activities that require your hands-on leadership.

Follow on Twitter: @MissionBio

CRISPR-based Platform for Real-Time Disease Detection

Trevor Martin

CEO and co-founder, Mammoth Biosciences

Over the past few years, technology has brought great advancements to healthcare, especially with regard to personalized medicines and targeted therapies. But not nearly the same amount of attention and focus has been brought to disease detection and diagnostics—a global market worth over $45 billion. The irony is clear: diseases cannot be adequately treated without having first been accurately diagnosed.

While finishing my PhD in biology at Stanford University, I embraced this challenge. I brought together a world-class team of scientists from both Stanford and Berkeley to leverage new technological advancements in CRISPR so that we can democratize access to powerful diagnostics. Similar to how Google built a search engine for the internet, Mammoth Biosciences has used CRISPR to build the search engine for biology. Our CRISPR-based platform can search and find nucleic acids that are indicative of disease in samples ranging from blood to saliva.

Using proprietary CRISPR technology licensed exclusively from the University of California, and further CRISPR technologies developed in-house, we're creating easy and affordable tests that allow for fast, simultaneous detection of multiple conditions, from common infections to cancer. Our vision is to create a test as simple as adding a liquid sample to a disposable strip and reading the result through Mammoth's app. In under an hour, we want people to be able to know the status of their health on their terms and in the privacy of their own home.

This will change our healthcare system as we know it. Our company is exploring various methods for delivering CRISPR-based disease detection tests, one of which could be a disposable test strip, which could detect anything from common infectious diseases (like flu) to cancer. Imagine: no more visits to the doctor to check your child for strep before he or she goes back to school, no more waiting at the ER for bronchitis results, and no more disparity between people who can and can't afford checkups at the clinic. With this test, people will gain access to knowledge about their own health and ultimately take back control over this costly part of the healthcare system.

Beyond having an impact in the US, Mammoth has the potential to change how hospitals and clinics work all around the world, especially in the developing world where doctors have limited access to advanced medical equipment. In contrast to equipment that's expensive and cumbersome to transport, Mammoth's test will not require refrigeration or instrumentation. That means doctors can go straight to the point-of-care and diagnose in real-time. This is essential during massive disease outbreaks, like Ebola, where the disease is highly contagious, transmits rapidly before symptoms show, and takes up to three days to diagnose in a lab setting. Ultimately, the faster the diagnosis, the faster the treatment response will be, and the closer we are to making a healthier world.

Mammoth could also improve the population's health by preventing disease outbreak in agriculture. By using Mammoth's proprietary CRISPR technology, partners could test for E.coli outbreaks or other food-borne illnesses before products reach grocery store shelves. Even in restaurants, workers could take a single swab of the kitchen counter to test for food safety. Soon, Mammoth will dramatically accelerate the detection process for new, unknown outbreaks and change the narrative when it comes to the world's most-feared pandemics.

Q&A with Trevor Martin

What brought you to this career?

During my early academic career, I recognized an opportunity to make an impact and give back through computational biology. Since then, the field has matured, and while there is certainly still potential, the field captured that same spirit of limitless possibility and no-holds-barred innovation that I felt in the early days of that work. The nascent field of synthetic biology and of CRISPR, pioneered by Jennifer Doudna's lab at Berkeley, was an obvious candidate for its huge potential in a wide variety of fields beyond gene editing. What makes building Mammoth such an exciting part of my career is the company's work to utilize CRISPR for the democratization of both diagnostics and the CRISPR platform itself—and building a team of individuals who are driven by this mission.

What are the potential drawbacks?

Our intent is for people to know as much about their health as possible. However, there are cases where we need to be careful about how this information is delivered. For example, tests that detect cancer will be more useful if provided in a more clinical setting, where healthcare professionals can communicate next steps and support. We always want individuals to understand and be comfortable with how to act on the information they just received.

How can we future-proof our career?

As new types of jobs are created and existing jobs evolve, the most critical skill someone can possess is to be adept at embracing new ideas and skills. Increasingly, education is not something that should be relegated to ivory towers but a core part of career development.

If you had a million dollars, what would you invest in?

The global disease detection market is worth over $45 billion. At Mammoth, we're focusing on the healthcare aspect but there are many other verticals in this area, including agriculture, oil and gas, and forensics. Given the potential impact, I'd continue to invest in technologies that make detecting disease fast and accessible and also apply them to markets outside of healthcare.

Follow on Twitter: @martintrevor_

LAB TESTING FOR PRECISION MEDICINE AND LOWER COSTS

Brian Caveney
MD, JD, MPH

ENTERPRISE-WIDE CHIEF MEDICAL OFFICER, LABCORP

Laboratory testing is often forgotten in healthcare discussions. It only accounts for a tiny portion of the money we spend on healthcare, but it is extremely impactful on diagnoses and outcomes.

In all the discussion of big data, and bridging the gap between claims and clinical information in EMRs, lab data is the one area of healthcare that is already structured and built for analytics and data mining. Lab-test data is specific, objective, and quantitative and little curation or natural-language processing is needed.

Lab data is important, and often under-appreciated, in our ability to measure quality and improve healthcare. A huge opportunity in the future, and one area we are excited about at LabCorp, is the idea that we can move from one-size-fits-all population medicine to precision medicine, providing individualized, customized interventions for each patient. Making precision medicine a reality will depend on better, more accurate biomarkers and genetic testing. It will help physicians make more specific diagnoses and better decisions about which medications they should, and could, use at the right dose.

In this way, lab testing can help manage pharmacy costs—the cost of medications being a focus of discussion in the media and among policy experts. Companion and complementary diagnostics can help a physician determine whether a patient's condition is likely to respond to a certain medication. Pharmacogenomic profiles can suggest whether a patient will metabolize a medication normally at the recommended dosage. And therapeutic drug monitoring can help determine whether the drug is circulating at an adequate concentration to be effective, and whether the patient has developed anti-drug antibodies to the medication. All of these can help optimize medication usage to achieve the desired clinical outcomes, bringing us one step closer to the idea of truly precision medicine.

LabCorp's diagnostics and drug-development businesses work together to realize those goals for patients, ordering physicians, and the pharmaceutical companies and biotech companies we serve. We see incredible opportunity to improve healthcare, and perhaps lower cost in the future, by using smarter laboratory testing to improve medication usage.

Q&A WITH BRIAN CAVENEY

What brought you to this career?

I come from a healthcare family and, ever since I was very young, I assumed that I was going to be a physician. But I've always been interested in the business and policy side of healthcare. I was in college in the early nineties when the country was in its last healthcare reform era, including the Clinton plan, the rise of HMOs [healthcare maintenance organizations], and other changes. I became very interested in health policy. Around this time, I was applying to medical school and became interested in either a combined MD/MBA or MD/JD.

Another event was serendipitous. When I was a faculty physician at Duke University and active in the North Carolina Medical Society, I found myself sitting next to a medical director from Blue Cross NC at a committee meeting. As we were chatting, she said, "We need someone like you at Blue Cross because the Affordable Care Act just passed. Our employer groups with health insurance do not understand its implications and how it applies to them. We need a physician who is able to explain the healthcare side and the policy side of the ACA."

I saw this as a great opportunity to apply my full background in a meaningful way and that's how I left clinical medicine and moved into a corporate environment. Everything that I've done since can be traced back to that one fortuitous conversation, including the amazing opportunity I had to move back to the provider side at LabCorp.

How can we future-proof our careers?

No matter how expert you are in your niche, realize that there is so much more to the fabric of the healthcare ecosystem than you can ever know. You have to be incredibly open minded to how the system works, how the different players within the system interact, how the money flows, and how the regulatory framework impacts the behavior of everyone in it.

Stay curious—you must follow industry news in order to stay relevant, and never stop learning about where you and your organization fit into the overall healthcare ecosystem. Medicine is now more complex than the human mind can process without help from machines, but it will be a long time before AI can replicate our empathy and contextual thinking.

Finally, pressure-test your own ideas. You will often come at a decision from the viewpoint of an expert in your niche, but it's important to also consider the perspectives of other stakeholders. When we are able to view any given topic within healthcare from multiple perspectives, we understand why it's so difficult to change the system, and why there is often no one "right" answer. Almost every proposed solution has trade-offs.

What do you believe in?

I've always been fascinated with learning, and often get made fun of for having three graduate degrees. I am a voracious reader, and I like to think about policy questions that impact healthcare. There may not ever be a silver bullet that will magically "fix" healthcare, but if we can be honest about some of the overarching ethical and political questions, use data to make sound decisions, and make steady, incremental progress, we can achieve greater financial stability and clinical improvements for patients.

Follow on LinkedIn:
https://www.linkedin.com/company/labcorp/

Treatment

The third step of the patient journey is treatment. The patient receives the prescribed treatment for his or her condition.

"I have loved the stars too fondly to be fearful of the night."

—Galileo

GENE-EDITING FOR ERADICATING DISEASE AND AI FOR EARLY INTERVENTION

Michael Bancroft

EXECUTIVE PRODUCER AND CO-HOST, GLOBALIVE MEDIA'S BEYOND INNOVATION

Gene-editing technologies hold astounding potential to improve the world for the better. While there has been some negative press, following the scandal with a rogue scientist in China altering human babies with CRISPR, this potential shouldn't be downplayed. It is theoretically possible that one day we'll be able to effectively eradicate many diseases by altering our genes to become resistant to them, saving countless lives and untold sums of money. It would also go a long way to alleviating the burden on the healthcare system by keeping people out of hospitals and freeing up professionals' time to focus on other pressing matters.

Some of these innovations don't have to happen before birth. For instance, a startup in Hong Kong called OPER Technology is developing nanotechnology to remove stem cells from a patient's brain, modify them to fight diseases such as cancer or Alzheimer's, and then reinsert them. There they can proliferate and eventually cure the patient of their ailment. What's crucial to advancing gene-editing technologies is to vastly increase the data we have about how our DNA, and genes in general, work.

There are several interesting startups working on this. One of them is Nebula Genomics, backed by the famed geneticist George Church. The company is paying people for the right to sequence their individual genomes and include that information in a giant database. Researchers can use it to study and develop treatments. Church believes that an understanding of our personal genomes will one day guide many choices we make in life, such as what to eat, how best to exercise, and how much sleep we need in order to ward off diseases we're predisposed towards.

One of the ways we'll leverage the greater amounts of data we're collecting about our genes, and our healthcare in general, is by using artificial intelligence and machine learning. We can deploy algorithms to greatly accelerate the study of healthcare data to unearth new treatments and pharmaceuticals that can address diseases. AI and machine learning can analyze the raw data being collected to figure out which combinations of compounds are more likely to treat disease effectively. This can help researchers reduce the time and cost of finding winning formulas. This is potentially transformative for the healthcare industry because it costs about $2.6 billion on average to develop a prescription drug, and there are countless billions spent on drug candidates that ultimately fail. That should mean that the retail price of drugs will fall, making these treatments more accessible to the patients who need them.

AI is also being used to spot diseases much earlier in their development in patients. A company called Cognetivity is using AI in a simple psychological test that takes 15 minutes, and the AI has been able to identify early signs of dementia and Alzheimer's. As a result, these patients can get the care they need when their brains are healthier to curb the effects of the disease. Ultimately, if AI can be used to identify health conditions much earlier, we may see pharmaceutical companies shift their focus to curing or treating early-stage diseases rather than late-stage ones. That would fundamentally change the way the industry operates towards more preventative, rather than reactionary, care.

Q&A WITH MICHAEL BANCROFT

What brought you to this career?

I learned to produce live news at the Los Angeles TV duopoly KCBS and KCAL. The news director at the time, Nancy Bauer Gonzales, gave me great advice. She said that if I wanted to be successful, I had to understand people and money, and suggested I get an MBA. I did just that and have an MBA in finance. Subsequently, my love for technology, innovation and entrepreneurship has grown. I have worked for broadcast networks including CBS, CNBC, ABC, BNN and Network Ten, and was an executive producer for Bloomberg TV.

What are the potential drawbacks of new technologies?

The overarching concern for many technologies is the way all of the data gathered is going to be collected, stored and used by the companies behind them. It's not hard to imagine a world in which we have no privacy whatsoever from technology companies, governments and nefarious agents who would seek to do us harm. It's also possible to envision scenarios in which we merely have the illusion of choice. Those who hold our data could understand, predict, and ultimately engineer our behavior based on an understanding of how we live each day.

There needs to be stricter regulation over data collection and privacy by governments, industry associations, and companies themselves. We don't want overly strict regulations that choke innovation and prevent data from being leveraged in a meaningful way, but there needs to be a more informed approach. On the flipside, consumers need to come to terms with the fact that there's no such thing as a free lunch. When you use technology, you're agreeing to provide information about yourself and your habits. We all need to be more thoughtful about the way we use technologies and consider which conveniences we actually need and how much we're willing to sacrifice for them.

Will AI steal our jobs?

There's plenty of hysteria over machines "stealing" our jobs, but much of it is overblown. AI is indeed becoming highly sophisticated and will automate many jobs, but we often don't consider the jobs that are created thanks to the added productivity that machines generate. For example, AI might automate some repetitive, procedural-style office jobs, but the company that implements it may open up new locations or launch new products with the money it saved, creating jobs at the new locations or in the product design team.

Ultimately, the best way to future-proof your career is to continually learn new and diverse skills that can be applied in many different roles.

Follow on Twitter: @MBancroft80

Dr. Kevin Campbell, FACC

CARDIOLOGIST AND MEDICAL EXPERT FOR
WNCN AND CBS MORNING NEWS

Before stethoscopes, doctors looked at the signs and symptoms. They would put their ear over the patient's chest. Once we had the stethoscope, we could hear what was going on in each chamber of the heart. We could listen to the rhythm and listen to what the valves were doing. And it changed the world.

One of the most significant issues in healthcare is data management and medication. When I was a cardiologist at Duke University and UNC, nurses and physicians spent a lot of time processing data. It was very labor intensive. Sometimes, it took me six weeks to get data from a pacemaker and defibrillator and then act on them. By that point, the data was obsolete and the potential life-saving period negated.

And that's where PaceMate™ comes in. PaceMate created a software program to take that data, process it with artificial intelligence within 15 minutes, and combine it with the expertise of nurses and doctors to provide real-time medical decisions. This is where doctors are most effective. When you get a PaceMate, your doctor will give you a machine that sits beside your bed that connects to your device by Bluetooth. It will check that machine every time you go to bed, or every time you walk by. If there is an abnormality, it sends that information to the manufacturer, whether it's Medtronic, Boston Scientific, Abbott or Biotronik and sends that information to the cloud.

Our artificial intelligence will flag the data as red, yellow, or green. Red flags that action is required, yellow flags that something looks abnormal and green is ordinary. Our technicians than looks at the data, validates and verifies for accuracy, and sends a text or email to the physician to flag abnormal signs. Your doctor or nurse then downloads that data, looks at it, and makes relevant, real-time recommendations. Once that is recorded, the information is scanned back into the electronic medical records.

It makes a huge impact to a patient. From a healthcare economics standpoint, we are preventing repeat hospitalizations for heart failure or strokes, and significantly decreasing healthcare costs.

Q&A WITH KEVIN CAMPBELL

What brought you to this career path?

I studied abroad at Oxford University [as an under-graduate] and came back with a strong global view. I knew I wanted to go into medicine, so I went to medical school to become a cardiologist. I started to notice things within the medical system or the operation process that separated doctors from patients. So I became a sideline entrepreneur and started working with tech firms and investors to create devices and software that can help bridge that gap and make a better experience for both patients and doctors.

Over time, I became engaged with the national media and worked with multiple outlets, including Fox News, CNN, CNBC, MSNBC, and CBS national. I would do a healthcare news commentary of the day and provide my two cents on healthcare policy. I became a sort of national media personality and realized that maybe I can make more of a difference by leaving medicine to focus on making medicine better.

When I retired from medicine, the first thing I did was volunteer and travel. A group of physicians, nurses, and I would sail on a 47-foot catamaran to the remote islands of Fiji and provide free medical care. Many of the locals have never seen a doctor, and it was a fantastic experience. We visited an island called Matiki, where they collected water from rain barrels and used solar power because they didn't have access to electricity. At the end of two weeks on the island, the locals welcomed me as an official chief of the village or Ratu, a huge honor. The Fijians taught me what medicine was about. Before that, I had gotten lost in insurance and electronic medical records.

What have you learned?

1. To be an effective leader or manager, understand that people respond differently to different leadership styles. Some people need coaching, some need autonomy. Learn to understand what each individual needs, and customize your approach accordingly.

2. Listen more and talk less. There is a whole lot that we can learn if we just listen.

3. Know what you know, know what you don't know, and find out how you can learn what you don't know. I've become a pretty good businessman but there are some things I need to know to be more effective. So I'm going back to school to get my MBA.

What tips do you have for working with the media?

Be in the right place at the right time. I got into media because there was a very famous basketball coach who had a sudden cardiac death. I did not participate in his treatment (he was in a different town) but I was in the middle of setting up the defibrillator, a machine that prevents sudden cardiac death, in the operating room. Journalists came and asked me to discuss this situation, so I talked about how important it was to be aware of your risk factors for heart disease. That story ended up not only in the local news but also the CBS network. From then on, producers started to call me and asked me to go on the show regularly.

My advice is be relevant and be timely. Understand the difference between an evergreen story and a story that is burning hot today. Know how to pitch yourself, and ultimately, build a brand. My brand, if you look through all my materials, is about putting the patients first. And ultimately, be relatable and make fun of yourself on air. Once, I was on Fox News for an exercise and diet segment and I had texted the host a video of me trying CrossFit back in the day. In the video, I was dying—my face was red and it looked like I was going to pass out. She let me know that they would most likely make fun of me. At the end of the segment, they played the video of me working out. I'm a physician but I have the same challenges as anyone—I needed to lose weight and I probably looked funny doing so. Make fun of yourself in a way that humanizes you but doesn't reduce your credibility.

Follow on Twitter: @Drkevincampbell

EDITING DNA TO FIX GENETIC DEFECTS

Dr. André Choulika

CEO AND CHAIRMAN, CELLECTIS

The expression "it's in my DNA" is commonly used to indicate the deepest inscription of who we are—but that's about to change. Our cells are no longer our genetic destiny. The ability to edit DNA in our cells not only frees us from a defined fate, but also opens the gate to an unknown world. As someone who helped to pioneer gene editing over 30 years ago, I consider it to be the next transformative step in medicine, with the potential to completely reshape it in the very near future.

The ability to edit genes offers the potential to fix any genetic defect in cells. It provides the possibility of treating people by curing the roots of diseases, instead of merely treating the symptoms. In the twenty-first century, humans are going to be able to erase unhealthy mutations in their DNA, and this could be the end of some genetic diseases and potentially the beginning of a new page in the history of humankind.

Gene editing is entering our lives today through game-changing applications. The first application, which has already changed lives, is gene editing for fighting cancer. While it's clear that T-cell therapies are coming to the forefront of cancer treatment with the FDA approval of Novartis's KYMRIAH® and Kite's YESCARTA®, both of these autologous products focus on leveraging a patient's own T-cells to create cancer treatments. This has serious constraints, including high pricing and limited market access, highlighting the need to personalize medicine on a larger scale.

Cellectis introduced the transformative idea of editing the genes of healthy T-cells to make them "off-the-shelf". In this way, patients don't need to provide their own T-cells to generate the product. "Off-the-shelf" T-cells, also named allogeneic, can be manufactured on an industrial scale, getting to patients faster, even for those that are lacking healthy—or any—T cells within their bodies. It's also more cost-effective. The ability to edit genes has the potential to free us from using patient-derived cells and would allow us to simply grab a treatment for cancer out of the freezer whenever a patient is in need.

Furthermore, allogeneic products can be available for all patients globally, including those who are unable to produce autologous CARs (chimeric antigen receptors) in countries where the technology is not yet available.

There are also lower logistical complexities and associated costs, as allogeneic products can potentially be shipped within a day worldwide and have the potential to reduce the final cost. Re-dosing is even possible with this approach, which contributes to a patient's overall survival.

Cellectis has already seen very promising results with UCART19, our first therapeutic product candidate—having dosed patients in compassionate care cases in the UK in November 2015 and May 2016. They were the first patients helped by gene editing. Now, this product candidate is in clinical trials under Servier and Allogene Therapeutics, Inc. through a licensing agreement. Recently, data was presented at ASH 2018, a premier industry conference, which showed the continued progress of UCART19 in phase 1 clinical trials, for both pediatric and adult ALL (acute lymphoblastic leukemia) patients. We are pleased to see continued progress for UCART19 under the management of our partners.

The initial results obtained with gene-edited CART therapies have been spectacular. While there are challenges in tackling other genetic inborn diseases, I'm sure they will be overcome in the next decades. The promise of "off-the-shelf", universal CAR T-cell therapies is enormous, especially for people living with certain forms of blood cancers. Additionally, since patients would be immediately dosed with allogeneic products, these treatments would be more accessible than the autologous treatments currently on the market.

Q&A WITH ANDRÉ CHOULIKA

What is the most interesting story that happened to you?

Molecular genetics has been at the center of my life for over 35 years. Over time, I became accustomed to analyzing progress with detachment. Our first therapeutic product candidate, UCART19, was first given to a patient in 2015 and my scientific mind worried about a whole series of things—not least the safety of the patient. Everything went well and the patient was cancer-free one month later. Six months after that, the story broke in the press. When I saw the news on TV, I saw the face of the young patient smiling and playing happily. This raised a deep emotion in me and sparked a passion to help more patients. At that moment, I understood the purpose I'd been working towards my whole life.

Why did you decide to focus solely on gene editing?

In the early 1990s, I was doing research at Institut Pasteur, playing with the first gene-editing tool, Omega. Omega was naturally occurring DNA scissors discovered by Prof. Bernard Dujon, who was my teacher. A virologist by training, I was working on a mouse leukemia retrovirus, the Moloney murine leukemia virus. I decided to introduce the target DNA sequence of Omega into this virus that was recombined. After I infected mice cells with this recombinant virus that, like HIV, integrates into the host genome, I introduced the infected cells. What I saw left me flabbergasted. The virus popped out of some of the host cells from their DNA. It was an incredible outcome that could have a huge impact on a number of diseases.

We immediately met with the patent department of Institut Pasteur. In 1992, we filed for the first patent on nuclease-based gene editing and included our vision on how this discovery could change the world. Since then, I've remained dedicated to my life's mission of using gene editing towards curing disease. Three decades later, we have good insight on how to potentially cure some forms of leukemia. I will probably need a second life to see my dreams of the early 1990s fulfilled, but it has been a fantastic journey.

Follow on Twitter: @cellectis

VIRTUAL REALITY FOR PTSD TREATMENT

Deborah C. Beidel
PhD, ABPP

FOUNDER AND DIRECTOR, UCF RESTORES®

UCF RESTORES® was founded to change the way the world views, understands and treats post-traumatic stress disorder (PTSD). Following the development of our three-week intensive outpatient program—the first of its kind in the United States—we have seen incredible success with participants, ranging from veterans and military personnel on active duty to first responders and the survivors of mass shootings.

We use virtual reality (VR) as part of our exposure therapy approach, and until now we've relied on a third party for the technology. Now, with funding from the US Department of Defense, we are developing our own, proprietary VR technology. This will allow us to precisely recreate each patient's traumatic scenario, taking the personalization of treatment to a completely new level.

From a treatment perspective, this is a game-changer. The closer you can bring someone to their traumatic event, the more effective the treatment will be. With our own technology, we will be able to recreate every element of the patient's perspective—including sights, sounds and smells—within a matter of hours. Beyond our ability to help people suffering from PTSD gain back control over their lives, we will have the power to help eradicate the stigma that surrounds the disorder as our program continues to grow and gain public awareness.

When UCF RESTORES first started providing PTSD treatment, we offered a 17-week outpatient program developed for veterans of the Vietnam War. As we applied it to the treatment of veterans from Afghanistan and Iraq, the program was successful. But it relied heavily on traditional outpatient exposure therapy and was very time intensive. While the program was working well for veterans, there was a concern that it would not work for active duty personnel; 17 weeks was simply too long for them to be out of pocket.

I was presented with the challenge of condensing a successful 17-week program. We settled on 21 days, as that time frame would allow us to deliver the same program without losing any of the critical ingredients. Many people thought it was crazy to try and implement such an intensive treatment for combat-related PTSD.

Exposure therapy carries the risk of taking an emotional toll on participants, as you're recreating the scenario that caused their trauma and having them imagine that event over an extended period of time. There was concern that it would lead to increased suicidal tendencies or substance abuse.

However, we took incredible care in developing this program and our unprecedented success rates speak to that—66% of participants with combat-related PTSD and 76% of first responders no longer meet the diagnostic criteria for PTSD following treatment. Our approach to treatment, combining emerging technology with one-on-one and group therapy sessions, has changed the game for those impacted by traumatic events.

We live in an age of terror and turmoil—both domestically and abroad—and, while it's so important to remember those who lost their lives, we can't lose sight of the hidden victims behind the scenes. So many of our veterans, active duty military and first responders, are suffering. My team is working tirelessly to help them take back control and restore a sense of normalcy in their day-to-day lives. The only silver lining to be found in the trauma caused by ongoing wars and the near-daily mass shootings is the ability to provide the front-line heroes, who dedicate themselves to saving the lives of others, with the help they need.

PTSD knows no boundaries—it affects people of all nationalities, beliefs and walks of life. As UCF RESTORES continues to raise awareness and scale up—statewide and nationally—I believe we'll be able to change how the world approaches the treatment and understanding of the disorder.

Q&A WITH DEBORAH C. BEIDEL

What brought you to this career?

On October 2, 2006, Charles Carl Roberts entered a one-room schoolhouse in the Amish community of Nickel Mines, Pennsylvania. He told the boys to get out before lining up 10 young girls, shooting each of them in the head at point-blank range and, ultimately, killing himself. On that day, I was serving as the chief psychologist at the Penn State Milton S. Hershey Medical Center. Half of the girls ended up in our emergency room and I spent the following months working through the aftermath. I cried with the families, dealt with the media and spent a lot of time with the first responders and medical personnel that responded to and treated the victims, all of whom were affected by this horrific, tragic event.

I will never forget the acts of courage and resilience that stood boldly in the face of this tragedy. There was the eldest girl, who stepped forward and said, "shoot me first," in an attempt to buy time for the younger girls. There were the women from that community who, on the night of the shooting, took food to the wife and children of the man who had murdered their daughters. And there was the population of Nickel Mines, who represented more than 50 percent of the people at Roberts' funeral. The emphasis placed on restoration and reconciliation in that community was unforgettable. Following that event, I knew I would be devoting the rest of my career to understanding trauma, as well as its aftermath, and doing my absolute best to advance its treatment.

Was there a tipping point?

The morning of the 2016 Pulse nightclub shooting, I got a call from the City of Orlando Fire Department, asking for our help for first responders on the scene of the massacre. In the year that followed, we saw more than 45 first responders, as well as survivors and victims' families, all of whom were in deep distress and suffering from PTSD. As we worked through our intensive outpatient program with each participant, we realized the need for more customizable VR scenarios. Until then, our participants had primarily been veterans and active-duty military personnel, and the [VR] scenes we had at our disposal were tailored to their experiences. They included IED (improvised explosive device) explosions and village gunfire attacks. We didn't have visuals that would work for the Pulse participants. While we were still able to successfully treat the victims, the visual VR component of our treatment was limited.

What advice would you give others?

Drop the jargon. It can be really difficult to get your point across if you speak a technical language, especially in a field like mine. Psychologists are trained to speak in terms of "probability of significance," qualifying what we do and looking at the potential limitations of studies, but the public wants to know the bottom line. I've had to figure out how to communicate my mission and vision in a way that resonates with others.

Follow on Twitter: @UCF_RESTORES

LASER TREATMENT OF PERIPHERAL ARTERY DISEASE (PAD)

Jeffrey Kraws

PRESIDENT, RA MEDICAL SYSTEMS

More than 200 million people worldwide[1] suffer from peripheral artery disease (PAD). It's a common circulatory problem in which plaque builds up in the arteries and reduces blood flow, causing severe pain and cramping in the lower extremities. PAD is the leading cause of leg amputation in the United States and, for too long, patients haven't had access to effective, economically viable alternatives.

That situation needed to change and so Ra Medical Systems developed a minimally invasive excimer laser called DABRA. DABRA is a tool used by physicians that reduces plaque into its fundamental chemistry, such as proteins, lipids, and other chemical compounds. This eliminates blockages by essentially photoablating [removing tissues by irradiating] them without generating potentially harmful particulates. It allows for a less painful procedure and a quicker recovery time for the patient. Most importantly it restores blood flow, and in many cases, directly avoids the need for amputation.

Peripheral artery disease is responsible for approximately 240,000 amputations every year[2]. Nearly one-quarter of these patients die within 30 days, and almost half within a year[3] of their amputation. Now, thanks to DABRA, these patients have new hope for retaining their legs and their lives. It's a quick, less-painful procedure performed in an outpatient setting.

Q&A WITH JEFFREY KRAWS

How can we future-proof our careers?

Look for problems within the marketplace and find a solution. If there is already a solution, find a better, safer and more efficient one. Don't be afraid of change. It's important to remember that problems and solutions consistently change. As a result, you must continue to adapt and grow.

What principles have guided you?

You can't always guarantee that you will be smarter than the competition, but be sure to stay disciplined and focused, trust your gut, and always strive to work harder than them. Everyone gets 24 hours a day, but it's up to you to choose how you spend them. I spend my 24 hours consistently learning and always striving to be better.

Follow on Twitter: @Ra_Medical

A NONINVASIVE TREATMENT FOR NON-MELANOMA SKIN CANCERS

Joseph C. Sardano

CEO, SENSUS HEALTHCARE

Superficial radiation therapy (SRT) provides a noninvasive, cost-effective treatment for non-melanoma skin cancers and keloids [raised scars] to patients all over the world. It is virtually painless and doesn't involve cutting, bleeding, stitching or anesthesia. There is also no risk of infection or scarring and no need for reconstructive plastic surgery. This is a game-changer for both patients and doctors. Not only does SRT offer comparable cure and recurrence rates to that of Mohs surgery, but it also allows for value-based care, which is where our healthcare system is headed today.

With SRT, we are providing patients with a non-surgical treatment option that uses painless, low-dose radiation. It only goes skin deep to destroy cancer cells—without damaging healthy tissue—and gives an aesthetically pleasing look and feel, as well as allowing patients to continue their lifestyles with little downtime post-treatment. This is particularly important for elderly patients, many of whom have diabetes and cardio-vascular disease, which makes them poor candidates for surgery. Additionally, patients with keloids have scars that can significantly impact their physical appearance and cause self-consciousness, anxiety and depression. All in all, SRT offers patients another option in the battle against skin cancer and keloids.

When the original developer of superficial radiation therapy (SRT) decided to sell us the rights, it was a good feeling because he had confidence and trust in the Sensus team to share this great technology that people needed. This has been something that has stuck with me since day one and continues to be the driving force behind SRT and helping treat people with skin cancer and keloids.

Q&A WITH JOSEPH C. SARDANO

What brought you to this career?

With more than 30 years in healthcare management, it had been a lifelong dream of mine to launch Sensus Healthcare with my best friends. Our mission was to provide highly effective, yet noninvasive, treatment options for both non-melanoma skin cancers and keloids. There are so many patients all over the world who are "surgically fatigued." Mohs surgery, as the current gold standard of treatment, just doesn't work for them or allow them to have a better quality of life. I greatly admire, respect and value the strong work ethic, integrity and insights that the Sensus team has to offer. All of this is ultimately what led me to create this company.

Follow on Twitter: @SensusHealth

REGENERATIVE TECHNOLOGIES FOR DAMAGED TISSUE

Robert S. Kellar

CHIEF SCIENCE OFFICER, AXOLOTL BIOLOGIX

At Axolotl Biologix, we have regenerative membranes and fluid products that are currently being used to treat patients where repair and regeneration is needed. Additionally, as the chief science officer (CSO) at Axolotl Biologix,[4] I am leading my team to develop next-generation technologies. These will allow us to create biomimetic skin scaffoldings, replacement blood vessels and even heart patches that will be a perfect match for the patient.

In the future, we plan to enhance our regenerative fluid with the addition of tropoelastin, a water-soluble version of elastin which can help to signal cells to promote repair and regeneration, and can be fabricated or incorporated into the extracellular matrix to give a stretchy characteristic to the tissue. This is important because the body quits making elastin as it ages. That's one of the reasons why we have wrinkles in aging skin, cardiovascular diseases, and even sports injuries. Our future solutions will help to return elasticity to damaged tissue, providing a better patient outcome.

With these breakthroughs, we can continue to provide physicians with new treatments to help promote wound healing, facilitate coverage and healing of burns, and much more. We anticipate that, with time, our breakthrough technologies will afford us the ability to fabricate a long list of biomimetic replacement tissues and potentially whole organs.

Q&A WITH ROBERT S. KELLAR

What brought you to this career?

After receiving my PhD from the University of Arizona, I jumped into a corporate career in the biotechnology and medical device industry. After a decade, I returned to academia to work with students. It was a big leap of faith, but it was also the biggest turning point in my life because I was helping to shape young minds who will change the future of medical research. Now, I am fortunate enough to teach university students and still develop emerging medical technologies with companies such as Axolotl Biologix.

What did you learn from your early corporate experience?

At Advanced Tissue Sciences (ATS), I worked as a research scientist and project manager, and ultimately in business development after the company had filed for bankruptcy. As the only remaining scientist, I had to find a home for as much of our technology as possible, and then liquidate all remaining assets. This period solidified my understanding of how important careful business management was for the future of a company. Having really cool technology wasn't enough. Following this experience, I went to work for a well-established medical device company, W. L. Gore & Associates, where I was able to learn first-hand how to wisely and responsibly run a business.

How can we future-proof our careers?

As a scientist, researcher and university educator, I know how quickly the biotech industry changes, so I think it is imperative to be constantly learning. New ideas and discoveries are made every day, so you need to keep an open mind to facilitate forward momentum. I am fortunate to work with incredibly talented young students whose questions open up new perspectives and spark creative solutions every day.

Follow on Twitter: @axolotlbiologix

Lifestyle Change

The fourth step of the patient journey is lifestyle change. Once the patient is home, he or she will make life changes to heal faster and to prevent readmission.

"If you wish to make an apple pie from scratch, you must first invent the universe."

—Carl Sagan

Dr. Bertalan Mesko

DIRECTOR, THE MEDICAL FUTURIST INSTITUTE

Digital health will make me, the patient, the point-of-care. This is one of the most significant milestones and breakthroughs in the history of medicine. Since the dawn of medicine, there has been an ivory tower. Only medical professionals can assess data, information, and technologies. There is no script or manual for the patient and the physician has the key. They open the gate, they let us in, they tell us what to do. Then we, as the patient, go home and only half of us comply with the therapy prescribed. It's an incredibly inefficient process.

Now it's different. Because it is the twenty-first century and we have new advancements in technology, a rise in social media, Amazon, crowdsourcing, and access to information, we are no longer in an ivory tower. There is no hierarchy. And because of this, we are becoming the point of care. Wherever we are, we want to get the best diagnosis and the best treatments. We should have an accessible, personalized, preventive, customized and humanistic patient journey.

As a researcher and physician working in this field for 10 years, I realized that I had to test everything out there to help patients, physicians, and policymakers genuinely understand where digital health is headed. I've tested health sensors, online platforms, and genetic tests. I've tried out a full-genome sequencing service. During my journey, I've tested and shared what I've learned from testing each product. I've learned what medications I have a sensitivity for, and the conditions for which I'm at increased risk.

I've also tested and shared what it means to interpret large amounts of data, with and without a partnership with my primary care doctor. I've shown people what it means to track sleep, and how to use a smart alarm so that you wake up at the best time and feel immediately energized. I've researched, and shared, what kind of bacteria live in my digestive system and what type of diet will be beneficial for me based on the four kilograms of bacteria detected.

I've tested more than 120 digital health technologies to truly become the patient of the future. I've tested some great devices, and some awful gadgets. One sleep tracker included a sleep mask. My wife loved it because when I turned it on, a green light came out of my forehead! She couldn't sleep for hours because she was laughing so hard. I believe there's real value in testing all the products out there to find out which ones work, which could benefit from behavioral tweaking, and which need to go back to the drawing board.

Accuracy is key. I need to be a physician, a researcher, and a geek, plus have the opportunity to get close to these technologies to analyze data and draw appropriate conclusions. It is very challenging to assess the accuracy of data and insights, as well as the efficiency of the products, without a blend of the right traits, training, and opportunity.

Privacy is a huge issue too. I am sure that many of the companies and products with whom I share my data are also selling that data. Even if I go out of my way to opt out of sharing data, my genomic information, though anonymized, could theoretically have been sold to third parties.

And then there's cost. I get these technologies for free but patients do not. Although the price of many of the technologies, such as genome sequencing or health sensors, has decreased over time, it is still not enough to provide access to low-resource regions. This leads to a socio-economic gap between those who can afford the technologies and live longer and healthier lives, and those who cannot.

Governments and major organizations are actively seeking help in these areas [of digital health] so we started to help them. Two years ago, I officially launched The Medical Futurist Institute, which conducts peer-reviewed research and provides consulting services in the field of digital health technology.

Q&A WITH BERTALAN MESKO

What brought you to this career?

I fell in love with science as a child when my mother bought me a children's encyclopedia. As I grew older, I decided to devote my life to medical science, particularly genetics. I went to medical school, then did a PhD in genomics. But I realized that I would rather supervise over 30 different branches or trends in technologies, rather than focusing on just one subfield of science. But there was no profession where I could achieve that, and that's how I became The Medical Futurist.

I took courses at Harvard's extension school, Singularity University, and many others. These courses helped me form the idea that I wanted to make a transition from the life sciences to social sciences and futuristic studies. About eight years ago, I started to build a team around the medical futurist concept. Our mission is to help people understand the context behind digital health technologies, from artificial intelligence to health sensors, and how it can impact their lives. We've been featured by *CNN*, *National Geographic*, *BBC*, *Forbes*, and *Time* magazine, among others.

Are politicians taking digital health seriously?

The Senate of Canada invited me to a public hearing about artificial intelligence and how it affects the healthcare space. It was inspiring how serious and dedicated the politicians were about bringing technologies into healthcare so that we can change lives. They were actively looking for help from outside experts. From that experience, I felt like the world had a bright future and that humanity truly has hope. And not long ago, I received an invitation from the World Health Organization to share a report on digital health. These are the amazing opportunities through which we can contribute to the evolution of digital health globally.

What are the potential drawbacks?

I am a very optimistic when it comes to digital health. But due to the current lack of regulations or inadequate regulations, the reluctance of physicians, or messy data, the field of digital health has a long way to go to overcome these setbacks.

Follow on Twitter: @Berci

Alfred Poor, PhD

EDITOR, HEALTH TECH INSIDER

My publication, Health Tech Insider, gives me access to C-level executives of major corporations such as Samsung, Philips, and Cigna, as well as the opportunity to meet founders of small startups and researchers from university labs. This gives me a perspective on the health tech industry that few have. Most people in health tech companies are busy developing their products and growing their businesses, whereas I have the luxury of floating above. That gives me a broad insight into the current state of the industry and where it might be headed.

I see many important shifts as a result of technology. One important change is the fitness trackers market shifting from consumer to enterprise. When a consumer buys a fitness band, it costs them money. When a large employer or insurance company or healthcare service buys 1,000 or 10,000 trackers for their employees, clients or patients, they see a real return on their investment that can be worth millions of dollars a year. One sign of this is the fact that Fitbit's most recent models were initially released only for corporate customers.

We're also seeing the benefits of the "quantified self" in healthcare. No longer are we just collecting data; artificial intelligence and big data analytics are turning this mass of numbers into actionable information. And we can see that healthcare systems are catching on. The recent American Heart Association guidelines for measuring blood pressure call for multiple readings, ideally not in a clinical setting but in the patient's home. Connected devices are making this easier for both patient and physician.

Remote patient monitoring is just one part of telehealth. It makes healthcare more accessible by shifting time and space for both patient and physician, and giving patients easier access to healthcare resources. This is not just a problem for sparsely populated areas such as the southwest; it's also a problem in Brooklyn. For the elderly or people of limited means, getting time off work, arranging for transportation, and enlisting the help of a companion can place enormous obstacles in the way of getting to a hospital or doctor's office. Remote monitoring can identify illness earlier so that treatment can start sooner. This results in fewer complications, better outcomes, and lower costs.

While we have access to some of the most amazing medical technology in the world, technology alone is not the answer. You need a sustainable system. The US healthcare system does not work well in sparsely populated regions. Our rural hospitals are closing at an alarming rate. And efforts that may increase the numbers of uninsured patients are likely to accelerate this effort. Patients will show up in emergency departments, and will have to be treated at the hospital's expense. We need more options that will give people affordable access to non-acute healthcare services.

Hospitals have enormous overhead, making individual services expensive. The $100 aspirin doesn't cost $100, but when you parcel out all the physical plant, employee, compliance, and insurance costs, it rapidly gets expensive. Having other, leaner options available with less overhead will help keep costs down. As a nation, we seem take the attitude that if we make unhealthy choices, someone will fix it for us. We need to continue the shift to a "wellness" attitude, with feedback systems that reward people for being healthy, rather than waiting to "fix" them when they get sick.

Q&A WITH ALFRED POOR

How can the US healthcare system be improved?

1. Encourage more states to pass laws that encourage telemedicine. New laws were passed by 34 states in 2017 but a lot of restrictions still persist. And since medical services—such as licensing—are regulated at the state level, this cannot be done at the federal level. The United States Department of Veterans Affairs has done a great deal to expand the use of telehealth technology but much more remains to be done[5].

2. Rapidly expand remote patient-monitoring services, not just for post-discharge situations, but to help monitor healthy individuals. Once-a-year "wellness" visits are inadequate—if they happen at all—and healthcare costs can be reduced by earlier detection and treatment of illness.

3. Make greater use of cognitive behavioral therapy (CBT) and gamification technology to encourage healthier choices. If we can make Facebook so persistently addictive, we should be able to create apps that engage individuals and encourage them to make better lifestyle choices.

4. Push for greater accuracy and reliability of wearable devices. When people were just using fitness trackers to

count steps, a 20% error rate was frustrating but not critical. Now that we're using the data for health and medical decisions, accuracy can be a matter of life and death.

5. Honestly evaluate connected devices for their impact on healthcare costs. While many help reduce costs, some classes of devices (such as infant monitors) can increase the number of unnecessary office and emergency department visits, thus pushing healthcare costs higher with no gain in better outcomes.

Follow on Twitter: @AlfredPoor

Aneela Idnani

COFOUNDER AND PRESIDENT, HABITAWARE

HabitAware helps people harness the power of awareness to create positive behavioral change. It was born out of necessity—my personal 20-year struggle with compulsive hair-pulling disorder, a mental health condition known as trichotillomania.

A few years ago, my husband caught me without eyebrows. So I had to share my hair-pulling secret and explain that it was the way I coped with stress, anxiety and boredom. I also shared how trance-like and automatic this soothing mechanism was for me—I just didn't realize until the damage was done. Then one day, as we were sitting on the couch watching TV, he grabbed my hand: he'd noticed I was pulling. I turned to him and said, "I wish I had something that notified me."

Fast forward to today. With my husband and two technically inclined friends, I built Keen. Keen is a smart bracelet that uses custom gesture detection to bring "keen" awareness to body-focused repetitive behaviors (BFRBs). These behaviors include hair pulling, skin picking (dermatillomania), nail biting and thumb sucking. BFRB affects 1 in 25 Americans but, because of the stigma, many hide like I did. Now, our Keen bracelet is giving hope to those people. It connects to a mobile app for a 30-second gesture-training process. When Keen senses a match to the gesture trained, it sends a vibration—a gentle "hug" on the wrist—reminding a wearer of where their hands are. With consistent practice, you can leverage the awareness Keen creates to retrain your brain and take control of these behaviors. This power of awareness is critical to making healthier choices.

Keen's innovation has the opportunity to create real-world change. The need for mental healthiness is finally being acknowledged by Western society. The mental health conditions we currently treat—hair pulling, skin picking, nail biting—negatively affect the lives of 20 million Americans and 70 million people in other first-world countries. As we adapt Keen to help people with other mental health conditions, we can help even more people.

The power of awareness that Keen provides helps people overcome disorders that consume physical and mental energy. When our Keen family makes the effort to build their awareness with Keen, they are able to overcome debilitating conditions. They are able to free this energy and translate it into their own "keens"—their own ways to change the world. We are helping thousands of people around the world take control of debilitating disorders of the kind I suffered from since childhood. It's exciting to bring this community together—we are not alone anymore!

Q&A WITH ANEELA IDNANI

What brought you to this career?

As a first-generation American, I grew up seeing my two immigrant parents work together at their own business endeavors. My mom practiced dentistry and ran her own practice and my dad traded products. We are Indian Sindhis and are descendants of the "business class." As such, I grew up feeding my creativity with various art projects and playing "office."

My career path has taken a lot of twists and turns. I started in accounting, because I loved the way T accounts just balanced. For someone with anxiety, it was very calming! But three years into working at a top audit firm, I found myself craving a creative outlet. I left accounting to travel and then continued my studies in art direction, copywriting and creative strategy. I then spent six years in top ad agencies in New York and Minneapolis, learning more about entrepreneurship than one could ever imagine.

What was the tipping point?

When we first started out, we weren't sure our idea would work, but rudimentary prototypes started helping me heighten awareness of when my hands started grazing to my eyebrows. We took still-premature prototypes to a conference held by the major non-profit for this mental health community, The TLC Foundation[6]. There, kids, parents and psychologists' eyes just lit up! That was when we knew we had to quit our day jobs and make this a reality. Immediately, we could see the excitement of this group of people who had for so long felt alone and ashamed. Finally, something had been created just for them! The mere existence of our tool for helping people overcome BFRBs was proof that this community of sufferers existed and mattered.

How can we future-proof our careers?

The biggest weakness is not in saying, "I don't know how to do that…" The biggest weakness is in saying, "I don't want to take time to figure that out." To "future-proof" your career, never lose your curiosity or desires for learning, for trying new things and solving problems.

What do you believe in?

My philosophy is that what I put out into the world with my thoughts and actions, I will receive. For a lot of my life, I was stuck in a vicious cycle of hair pulling and negative self-thought. It fed my decision-making and led my life path. The power of awareness of my hand movements has transcended to the power of awareness of my thoughts. I am happier because I believe good things are in my future and because I know that even if something bad happens, it is happening to bring me to a better place than I was before. When I was 17, I lost my dad to cancer. Now, 20 years later I am at peace with his death because I understand that his sickness led to so many great things in my life—including meeting my best friend and then meeting my husband through her introduction.

Follow on Twitter: @habitaware

AI ROBOTICS TO ALLEVIATE LONELINESS AND SOCIAL ISOLATION

Dor Skuler

CEO, INTUITION ROBOTICS

Did you know that some people over the age of 70 only interact with one person per week? It's a major problem in our society. Many older adults are dealing with loneliness and depression, and while I would love to say that people are stepping up and engaging more, it simply isn't happening. We asked ourselves—is there a way technology can help?

ElliQ is the answer. It's a tabletop device that pro-actively engages with people, getting them connected on social media, reminding them of their daily tasks, and encouraging them to learn and stay physically active. During the process of developing ElliQ, we realized that the technology had even bigger potential. If technology can use sensors to understand its environment, and be programmed to learn in order to make more personalized, proactive actions, we could completely change the way humans interact with machines.

Right now, tech products in our lives are based on a reactive model of interaction. You prompt, in whatever way, that a device needs to do something, and it may or may not respond the way you want it to. This has several drawbacks. For one, we need to learn how to use every piece of technology that comes into our lives! This is difficult for older adults, but also, as technology becomes more advanced, this may become more difficult for everyone. Second, it takes time and energy on our part, and may not even produce the result we want.

When we set out to develop ElliQ, the idea of the final experience was clear but how we were going to create it was much more complex. We had to understand the user, their personal preferences, and the nuances of the user's environment. And we had to find ways for the product to learn the user's goals and continue to refine its approach to achieving them. Most importantly, we had to assess all of the different ways ElliQ could create these interactions. It was during this development process, when we saw the incredible potential of multi-modal design, that we realized that this could apply to any device and so we began to develop our unique AI platform.

What we have created is a platform that any company can use, which transforms any machine capable of interaction into a "companion device"—a device capable of learning its user's preferences in order to proactively make decisions to support him or her. Your device will know what you want and need, and understand the different factors in its environment, in order to help you accomplish your goals. This will make our lives simpler and more enjoyable, and also provide huge benefits to older adults and people with disabilities.

Imagine if instead of having to ask your technology to perform a task, it simply understood what you were trying to accomplish and proactively helped? Every area in which technology can support our lives will become exponentially more personal and more effective—the possibilities are truly endless.

Q&A WITH DOR SKULER

What brought you to this career?

I started in the Intelligence Corps in the Israel Defense Force Unit 8200 before creating my first company, Zing Interactive Media. It was a venture-backed startup company in the field of mobile interactive media. Afterward, I served as vice president of business development and marketing at Safend, an endpoint security company. Then, I moved to Bell Labs in Alcatel-Lucent, where I built and ran businesses and was general manager of mobile security in the company's Enterprise Business Division. I then moved to a corporate role as VP of strategy and corporate development and founded a large-scale internal startup as SVP, general manager of CloudBand Business Unit, credited as one of the key factors behind the acquisition by Nokia.

I left Alcatel-Lucent with the goal of creating a startup with high social impact. Throughout my career, I enjoyed switching to domains where I'm not an expert but which are on the cusp of the latest technologies. Focusing on longevity was an important place to try and add value. My co-founders and I became passionate about helping older adults keep active and engaged, and avoid loneliness and social isolation—an epidemic in modern society—through a venture that's focused on celebrating aging rather than disabilities.

How can we future-proof our careers?

The future of work is unclear; we really don't know how things will play out and which jobs are "guaranteed." That said, understanding how you can utilize technology in order to enhance your current job is one way to proactively keep your role safe or be a leader in moving your field into the future.

Follow on Twitter: @dorskuler

MACHINE LEARNING FOR HEALTHCARE DATA

Dr. T. Greg McKelvey Jr., MPH

HEAD PHYSICIAN, ASAPP

Right now, healthcare decisions are not made with full information, let alone optimal intelligence. Providers make decisions based on anecdotes, statistics, or convenience. The net result is that we're not making the best possible decisions for every patient all the time. Up until recently, it was because we didn't have the data. But with advanced interoperability, we now have the data in front of us, and we have the machines capable of doing something with it. We have the ability to start learning from the data to make better decisions.

The ability to make better decisions based on massive data and computational intelligence is what we're here to solve. When I was the CMO at KenSci, our product is a software platform in the cloud. It is built for machine learning on healthcare data. It's very different than the cloud infrastructure platforms from Amazon, Google or Microsoft in that it is constructed only for healthcare. And healthcare is different because it has very specific terminology and patterns that make it very complicated. Healthcare data cannot be translated into another industry, and vice versa. We have done a lot to make sure that we can use that data safely, and that our platform enables usable and useful health-specific intelligence.

One of the things that differentiates us is that we've kept the system almost open source. We essentially use our platform not as a closed black box, but as a way to help clinical data science teams learn how to manage their own AI infrastructure and strategy. In particular, we're focusing on two specific places where we see the absence of effective prediction or risk stratification.

First, we are trying to understand the demand on the healthcare system so that we can better match demand with supply. We want to effectively and efficiently move patients through the healthcare system. We do that by projecting how many patients will arrive, how sick they will be, what type of care they will need, how long that will take, and where they will go next. Then we look at the risks. What are the risks of bad things happening along the way? We look at the entire acute care patient journey—from the operating rooms to recovery to post-acute care.

Second, we're focusing on population health, looking at what will happen to people in the more distant future. Rather than predicting behaviors over the next minutes or hours, we are looking over days, weeks, months and years to understand who is getting sicker, who needs a bit more attention, and how we can best manage whole groups of people despite limited resources.

Machine learning predictions can be uncannily accurate. One of the sets of machine-learning model outputs we provide helps emergency departments understand how many patients will show up in the near future. This helps them ensure they have enough staff, supplies, and beds on hand. There were a few times when we ran the models and pilots and it would predict that 14 patients were going to come in in the next hour. We thought something had gone wrong because there was no one in the waiting room! Then, all of a sudden, a pack of people would walk in. And as we counted them... lo and behold, there were 14!

Another model predicts which patients will go to the emergency department and then leave before seeing a provider. One time, it identified a patient with a 99% probability of leaving without being seen. With this, the emergency department proactively brought the patient in as a fast-track patient and conducted their first sets of vitals. After the first sets of vitals, the patient got off the table and walked out of the emergency department, now with the label, "left while being seen." The ED nurses referred to the model as "scary accurate"!

There are definite drawbacks, though. No matter how fancy your machine is, it is still just a tool. It's technology, and at the end of the day, the impact of using that technology is determined by how it is used, to what extent, and with what aim. People, process and policy problems cannot be solved with technology alone. Complex challenges in this industry are impacted by many different moving parts, agents and agendas. Health insurance will use healthcare data to optimize what healthcare insurance firms care about. Doctors will do the same. If we don't always keep in mind that we really should be solving challenges for patients, we will end up with unintended consequences.

Q&A WITH T. GREG MCKELVEY

What brought you to this career?

Two things happened around the same time that brought me to this path. The first was an experience as an intern early in my medical training. I was part of an electronic health record implementation, and I witnessed the gaps in the orchestration of the rollout. I remember thinking that physicians did not have adequate input into the design of the system. As a provider, it felt like it was detrimental to me rather than helpful, and certainly detrimental to the patients I was caring for.

Then shortly after the electronic health record rollout, out of nowhere it seemed, Amazon recommended a product to me that was actually very relevant! It was an excellent recommendation, and a light bulb went off. I realized that if that level of technology made its way into healthcare, it could create tremendous benefits. But if it were mismanaged the way previous technology implementations were, it could also create significant risk. So I started to learn more about the technology and informatics space. I went on to become chief medical officer at KenSci and am now at ASAPP.

What have you learned?

Even in the world of high technology such as healthcare data, big data, cloud computing, machine learning, people are still the root of everything. That includes the problems and the successes, and they are also the catalyst to helping us solve issues. If you see people as potential allies rather than obstacles to engineer around, you will get more information and you will tend to get to the right place more often.

What advice would you give others?

There's a quote by tennis legend Arthur Ashe: "Start where you are. Use what you have. Do what you can." And repeat. I think that's the answer for everything, from solving a small problem to overhauling an entire industry. I also think that ignorance is more of an enemy than evil. There is a maxim that captures this called Hanlon's razor and it says "never attribute to malice that which is adequately explained by stupidity." It's been very true for my life to this point.

How can we future-proof our careers?

Dr. Anthony Chang is a healthcare AI luminary and he said that "robots will not take your job, but somebody who knows how to work with robots will take your job." I think that's true. One aspect of staying "future-proof" is learning how to dance with automation. However, there are always going to be things that it won't do cost-effectively. The problem is that we don't know exactly what those things will be ahead of time. The only way that you can ensure you will be in a position to add value on top of what machines are taking away is to be able to adapt to new things really quickly. So the number one skill I would recommend is to learn how to learn.

Follow on Twitter: @DrGregMcK

A HEALTH INSURANCE PLATFORM FOR CUSTOMER CHOICE

Abir Sen

CEO, GRAVIE

Our healthcare system leaves a lot to be desired. A big part of the problem is that the end user, the consumer, has very little power or say in the system. For most of us in America, our health-insurance choices are made by our employers on our behalf. As a result, we get into this crazy situation where the HR department at someone's company has more say than the individual or their doctor about which hospital they can go to if they get sick, or what drugs they may or may not be prescribed.

Gravie, the company I lead and co-founded, changes this. Under our model, the employer gives the money that they are already spending on healthcare—which can be as much as $20,000 per employee per year—to the employee through our platform. The employee then uses those contributions to shop in our online marketplace with the help of a concierge service (which we call Gravie Care), to buy health insurance and other benefits tailored to fit their family's needs. In theory, each employee at a single company could end up with a completely different set of benefits.

One big problem with our current system is that no one thinks of the consumer as the customer. Insurance companies think of brokers as the customer and brokers think of employers (whose primary concern is often cost savings) as the customer. Consumers are just a captive audience that the employer brings to the table. This leads to an incredibly inefficient purchasing process. Insurers focus on keeping brokers happy, who in turn focus on keeping employers happy. A lot of golf is played. Consumer experience isn't necessarily discussed on the golf course.

Gravie's system gives the consumer the ultimate power—the power of the purse. In our model, if consumers don't like what they have, they can simply choose a different option next year. Their experience with a product or company, good or bad, can be shared with other consumers looking to make similar purchase decisions. In turn, insurance companies and other industry players now need to think of pleasing the consumer in order to get and keep them as a customer —designing products and services that address their needs and concerns. Just like in any other consumer industry, competitive pressures lead to product innovation. This in turn will improve the way the healthcare industry serves its true customers—people like you and me.

Q&A WITH ABIR SEN

Was there a turning point in your career?

At a previous company in its early days, we were approached by an insurance company executive who wanted to meet. I wasn't thrilled about going to this meeting. The company was located in a city that was difficult to get to and I didn't think the meeting would amount to much since we didn't sell to insurance companies. In addition, the vice president (of the United States) was visiting my home city the day prior to the meeting, resulting in all flights being put on hold until late in the evening. It meant I would reach my destination at 1:00 a.m. for a 7:00 a.m. meeting.

I thought about canceling the meeting or switching it to a call—but luckily, I didn't. It turned out to be one of the most important meetings in the life of the company. The insurance company became a big customer, and later played a large role in the successful exit of the company. This has happened to me throughout my career—big outcomes were driven by events which, at the time, seemed relatively inconsequential. It's deepened my belief that simply showing up is a big part of the startup battle.

What have you learned?

Crafting the right initial team is way more important than crafting the right initial solution. Across the four companies I have co-founded, none (none!) ended up with a business model that was the same as when the company was launched. The business model is not what makes the company. Rather, it's thoughtful, resourceful people that are determined to solve problems for an industry. The right team eventually experiments its way into the right model. Otherwise, things are a lot more painful.

Which are your principles?

I live by two principles, which are the same in everyday life as in my career. One, I have a "no jerk policy." I choose not to work or in any way associate with people who are jerks, even (especially!) when it is inconvenient or expensive. And two, I trust my gut more than my brain.

Follow on Twitter: @abirsen

Ongoing Care

The last step of the patient journey is ongoing and proactive care. The patient will manage his or her care in between doctor visits.

"Never doubt that a small group of thoughtful, committed citizens can change the world; indeed, it's the only thing that ever has."

—Margaret Mead

AN APP FOR ONGOING CARE

David S. Williams III

CEO, KAREN

Karen is transforming the interactions between patients, families and physicians by using technology to move from episodic, verbal exchanges of information in doctors' offices to ongoing conversations about care. These are delivered in the home and community and use text messaging, media, and data to paint a digital picture of patient experience between visits.

Because data is generated on an ongoing basis, the healthcare team can intervene immediately if a care plan is not being followed, thus avoiding costly emergency visits and hospitalizations. Karen has demonstrated significant impact in the number of interactions, clinical data points generated, and care plan adherence through the use of digital "Conversations." In three separate case studies with hundreds of participants, Karen resulted in the capture of more than 360 clinically relevant data points per patient per quarter and increased care-plan adherence by 68% during the three-month period.

When including text messages, photos, videos, and audio shared between family and providers, Karen Conversations drove more than 450 quarterly interactions per patient and led directly to an average of two intra-quarter adjustments in care plans. This means patients received better care because of the information they shared on Karen.

We have a groundbreaking new initiative underway. For industry, we are currently working on a machine-learning predictive algorithm. It will alert doctors and other interdisciplinary care professionals when frail elderly patients need an intervention to avoid emergency visits and hospitalizations. These alerts will give community care providers with information on how likely someone is to have an emergency episode.

Because Karen data can't be found in EHRs [electronic health records], the predictive algorithm will be based on longitudinal real-time data. This is data from real-world experiences that have led to hospitalizations—not claims data, incomplete or irrelevant medical evidence, or the unstructured recollections captured in physician's notes. In short, Karen provides greater access to care providers, more complete care, and improved outcomes.

Q&A with David S. Williams III

What brought you to this career?

My mother almost died having me and later, when I was 11 years old, she was told she had terminal liver cancer and only had six months to live. Rather than giving up, my mother wanted to live for her children, and she did. I grew up as a caregiver for her numerous health issues, thankful she was even alive. She ended up living until just before my 39th birthday. Once I graduated from college, I started management consulting to the healthcare industry with Deloitte. The light went on in my head that the challenges we had faced in aligning her care among providers and getting support weren't confined just to her. It was a systemic problem in the industry based on a paternalistic culture of "doctor knows best." In order for this to change, the culture had to change. And the most effective change agent is data—the right information delivered at the right time to the right person who can make the right decisions. Healthcare, believe it or not, is mediocre in that process.

How have you used Karen in your own family?

My son has severe autism and my wife and I used Karen to track his symptoms and vitals for three months. We learned that our son's aggressiveness (biting, scratching, etc.) and head-banging seemed to be related to an elevated heart rate. We shared this information with our doctor, who prescribed medicine to try to regulate it. The result was less aggressiveness and head-banging which saved family, teachers, and aides many bites, scrapes, and scratches, and our son from self-injurious behavior. It is amazing. The overall problem, however, is that doctors can't get this type of information from an electronic health record. They have to work with patients and families to make these types of breakthroughs.

What have you learned?

1. Sales cycles are going to be even longer than you think. Why? Time is money and startups need cash to survive.

2. Be wary of political agendas. Your technology may prove that other initiatives are failures rather than purported successes. Sidestepping the politics can mean a faster sale—not doing so can result in no sale, even when your product would perfectly serve patients' needs.

3. Take care of your mental and physical health. Building a company is an emotional rollercoaster. It impacts you and everyone you love so you have to take care of yourself to maintain a healthy life.

4. "OK" is not good enough. The idea of getting a tech platform "out there" before it's ready for primetime just to begin the process of getting feedback is a myth. Getting a bad product out there can have a lasting negative impact that can be difficult, if not impossible, to dig out of.

5. The rules are not the same for you. As a person of color, everything will be more difficult in a startup— especially fund-raising. Even if you have a strong entrepreneurial background with multiple exits and a great educational pedigree, it will still be hard to raise money.

How can we improve the healthcare system?

1. There is zero price transparency throughout the industry, which undermines a true capitalistic healthcare model. The only result can be oligopoly under current market conditions. If pricing were truly transparent, consumers could shop for better care by price and outcome as a ratio. Who wouldn't do that?

2. The culture needs to change. The "doctor as hero" complex is a bug, not a feature. Physicians need to be more collaborative and use their powers for the good of patients, not their egos. The non-cynical response is that doctors need actionable information because that's

how they can be at their best—analyzing issues and designing care plans to solve them.

3. Healthcare leaders must advocate for better interoperability between healthcare systems, with government entities allocating funds, much like meaningful use did for EHRs. This has to be done at the community level rather than for healthcare facilities. Given that 95 percent of care is delivered outside of healthcare facilities, imagine how much data is lost on care and what that translates to in poor outcomes.

4. Care programs have to be truly consumer-centric.

5. Stop trying to take healthcare away from people. While that seems obvious, there are cascading impacts from the uncertainty introduced in the market when current laws are threatened. Companies refrain from making medium and long-term investments because of uncertainty. Venture capital and private equity investors reduce their investments or prematurely sell their stakes in companies because of a fear that the underlying market assumptions will deteriorate their portfolio companies' economic models and valuations. Uncertainty kills investment, innovation, and meaningful progress.

Follow on Twitter: @yeskarenapp

Morris Miller

CEO, XENEX

Antibiotic resistance is responsible for the deaths of 700,000 people each year. That number is expected to skyrocket to 10 million deaths by 2050 unless action is taken. These deaths are caused by antibiotic-resistant pathogens like methicillin-resistant Staphylococcus aureus and vancomycin-resistant enterococci (VRE). We no longer have antibiotics to treat the infections they cause. The only way to combat this epidemic is to reduce the number of cases where antibiotics are needed. If you destroy the pathogens before they are transmitted to people, then infections are prevented. It's a paradigm shift in the way we think about antibiotic resistance and superbugs. If you kill the pathogens before they make people sick, you don't need antibiotics to treat the infections.

That's what LightStrike Germ-Zapping Robots accomplish. The robots use intense pulsed-xenon ultraviolet (UV) light that quickly destroys pathogens so that they can't reproduce, mutate, or cause infections. The robots are operated by a hospital's cleaning team and have proven effective against the most dangerous microorganisms, like Ebola and anthrax, as well as the most common (MRSA, influenza). Hospital employees clean the rooms—they remove trash and visible dirt/fluids and change the linens—and then bring in our robot to destroy pathogens that you can't see but which may have been missed during manual cleaning. Right now we are focused on healthcare—hospitals, surgery centers, long-term acute care facilities and skilled nursing facilities. But there are certainly other places where our robots could have an impact, including professional sports locker rooms, cruise ships and airports.

I think it's important to understand the enormity of the epidemic facing healthcare facilities today. Nearly 100,000 people die in the United States every year from healthcare-associated infections. That is more than 300 people dying every day from an infection they acquired during their hospital stay. Everyone knows someone who went to hospital to have a hip or knee replaced, seek treatment, or have a baby, and who contracted a scary (and sometimes deadly) infection. These infections are caused by microorganisms like *C.diff* (*Clostridium difficile*), MRSA (methicillin-resistant Staphylococcus aureus), and CRE (carbapenem-resistant Entero-bacteriaceae) that remain on hospital surfaces even after a room has been cleaned. They linger on tray tables, bedrails, doorknobs, OR [operating room] equipment, wheelchairs, and IV poles.

Some of the really scary ones—like *C.diff*—can live on surfaces for up to five months. Hospitals need more than two hours to properly disinfect a hospital room using traditional methods, but the germs that make people sick are becoming resistant to cleaning chemicals and antibiotics. In addition, financial pressure only allows hospitals to give cleaning team members 28–45 minutes to get the room ready for the next patient, when it takes over two hours for proper disinfection. That's what is so frightening. The germs have become resistant to antibiotics and we don't have the time to properly disinfect the rooms or have the drugs to treat the diseases they cause.

Infections happen to everyone, even healthy people in the prime of their lives—not just the elderly or people who are immuno-compromised or weak. Our mission is to stop the deaths, pain and suffering caused by healthcare-associated infections. If we can stop the infections and reduce the risk of antibiotic resistance, we can change the world. Hospitals using LightStrike robots are reporting 50, 75 and even 100% reductions in their infection rates. Adding LightStrike room disinfection to a hospital's comprehensive infection-prevention strategy (hand hygiene, antibiotic steward-ship, etc.) will make a difference.

We believe so strongly in the technology that we offer hospitals a no-risk program by which they can evaluate our technology in their facility at no cost. We provide robots and training for hospital employees at no cost, and then track utilization. We guarantee that the hospital will see a reduction in infection rates or else they can send the robots back. They only pay us when they've seen the agreed-upon reduction in infection rates. We did this for a hospital in New Orleans and they recently reported a 70% reduction in infection rates since they have been disinfecting rooms with LightStrike robots. That facility is using 16 of our robots and has expanded the program to other facilities in their system.

To date, LightStrike Germ-Zapping Robots have run more than 17 million cycles in hospital rooms. Using CDC statistics, that means that over the past five years, the robots have helped hospitals prevent 340,000 infections—and saved 37,000 lives. Conservatively, the average cost of treating a MRSA, *C.diff* or surgical site infection is $11,000 (per infection), so hospitals have saved $3 billion as a result of fewer infections. Preventing just a couple of infections pays for a robot and most hospitals report ROI in just a couple of months.

There's also the PR value, which can't be overlooked. Hospitals are now required to report some of the infections they cause—such as *C.diff*, MRSA and some surgical site infections. It means that consumers can go online and check out the infection rates for the hospital where they are going. Naturally, nobody wants a loved one to go to a hospital with high infection rates.

When we started the business, we were hoping that we could help hospitals get a 5–10% reduction in their infection rates. We were astonished when hospitals began reporting greater than 50% reductions—some experienced more than 75% reductions. We knew the technology had the potential to make a huge difference, but we had no idea just how enormous an impact it would have.

Q&A WITH MORRIS MILLER

What brought you to this career?

I started my career as an attorney at a law firm, and launched a company that was the first to publish Texas case law on CD-ROM. After selling the publishing company to Thomson Reuters, I wrote the first check and co-founded Rackspace. Eventually I started my own venture capital firm, which brought me to Xenex. When the Xenex founders approached me about their

Germ-Zapping Robot technology, I consulted with my father, a retired physician who specialized in internal medicine, about the technology's potential. I was shocked when he told me that being able to stop healthcare-associated infections could have more of an impact on humanity than his service to patients throughout his entire career. The Xenex founders, Dr. Mark Stibich and Dr. Julie Stachowiak, had a focused mission—to stop the needless pain and suffering and over 100,000 annual deaths caused by healthcare-associated infections. It was something I was proud to get behind and help grow.

What challenges do you face?

I once visited an infectious disease doctor at a world-renowned hospital and presented four peer-reviewed studies from hospitals. The hospitals had seen their infection rates plummet after adding our Light-Strike room disinfection technology to their cleaning protocols. Despite the evidence, the doctor didn't believe our robots could kill the germs that make people sick and help bring down the facility's infection rates. But she was willing to give LightStrike a chance because other interventions weren't working. Nine months later, she conducted her own independent, controlled trial. The results, which were recently published in the American Journal of Infection Control[7], showed that

C.diff infection rates fell 47% on the units where our robots were used for room disinfection. *C.diff* infection rates increased on the units that were not disinfected with our robots. The hospital deployed 12 robots and has continued to see reductions in their infection rates. While the story has a happy ending, it feels like we have to repeat the same process in every hospital.

Are there any potential drawbacks?

Preventing infections in a hospital requires teamwork—the facility's infection prevention and environmental services (EVS) team members must work together to develop and maintain a successful infection-prevention program. It's a huge misconception that the robots can do the work of the hospital's EVS team members. Our Germ-Zapping Robots are not replacing human jobs and they need to be part of a comprehensive infection-prevention strategy. Successful infection prevention requires a comprehensive strategy—hand hygiene, antibiotic stewardship, and LightStrike room disinfection.

What have you learned?

1. I once explained how our robot works to the CEO of a for-profit hospital, and how easily it can be integrated into the hospital's cleaning strategy. He told me I was

naïve. He said: "It's not flattering, but we make money even when we make people sick." Learning that hospitals profited from infections was something I never expected.

2. Be patient. Selling technology to healthcare facilities is complex and time-consuming. Many industries embrace innovation but in hospitals, even if you offer a technology that is statistically better than what they are doing and it can save them money, they may still take years to adopt it.

3. Patients must be responsible for their own safety. Check out the hospital where you or your loved one is going. If the hospital isn't using pulsed xenon UV disinfection technology, then find a facility in your area that is.

What advice would you give others?

The most important question to ask is, "why not me?" When I started my first company, I was rejected 168 times before I found my first investor. Be willing to be rejected, whether it's by an investor, a customer, etc. It's not a coincidence that the harder you work, the luckier you get.

Follow on Twitter: @xenexdisinfect

INVENTORY MANAGEMENT TO ELIMINATE PRODUCT WASTE

Carl Natenstedt

CEO, Z5 INVENTORY

There are thousands of hospitals in this country, even without counting the smaller facilities like standalone emergency rooms and doctors' offices. And if you go to the dumpsters out back, you will find piles of medical and surgical supplies that have been thrown out due to expiration. It all adds up to $5 billion worth of waste every year.

In my previous jobs, I visited lots of hospitals around the country, touring the facilities. I was constantly blown away by the amount of excess product hidden in every cubbyhole and desk drawer. Every single operating room is loaded with product. The worst room I've ever seen was totally disorganized and piled to the gills with boxes of stuff that was expiring or expired. It was managed by a procurement person who'd been at the hospital for over 50 years. She was never going to change her methods because she'd been doing the same thing for so long.

Other people who'd been in healthcare for much less time than her didn't have any motivation to change either. It needed someone on the outside, who was sick to their stomach at his visual reminder of consumption waste, to offer a solution. Nobody else was offering it, so I set out to make it and Z5 Inventory was born. Z5 Inventory's mission is to put that product to good use. We do it by moving supplies between hospitals within the same system, selling product from one hospital that doesn't use it to another that will, and donating the excess to charitable causes. Z5 uses predictive analysis and machine learning to anticipate product consumption to eliminate product waste in healthcare.

Imagine turning a $5 billion annual loss into savings. With these savings, hospitals can reduce costs and reinvest in their communities. What's more, we can keep perfectly good medical supplies out of landfills. Even if we can't find a destination for them in hospitals, we can get them to those in need. Z5 Inventory facilitates the donation of product to our hospitals' charitable partners and our own. We're proud to work with groups like Project C.U.R.E. and Cherish Uganda to provide life-saving medical and surgical supplies to communities that wouldn't otherwise have access to them. Every time I'm struggling to get a hospital to make this positive change, I remember that a child affected by HIV in Uganda could have been helped today by what we're doing, and it makes me fight twice as hard.

We're creating a real mindset change within the industry. We need to convince people that throwing all these medical supplies away isn't normal or even necessary. Providers can turn that loss into savings. And more and more of them are doing just that every day.

Q&A WITH CARL NATENSTEDT

What brought you to this career?

For me, wanting to be an entrepreneur started as a kid. I watched my dad start an entrepreneurial business during my formative years. I saw him build it as I grew up, and in high school I saw it fail. Understanding what that meant to the employees, the community and, of course, my father motivated me. It piqued my interest in startups and small business, but it also made me realize that, if I wanted to start a business, I had to do it the right way.

How did you go about it?

I got all the necessary training. I got a degree in finance, became a certified public accountant, and did 10 years in the public accounting sphere. In 1999, I knew a guy who knew a guy who happened to be a billionaire. He was looking to form an incubator for new businesses with big ideas. We had lunch on a Friday and I pitched him a tech-based healthcare supply-chain business. By the end of the dinner, we had a dozen ideas for the name of the company sketched out on a napkin. At the bottom, he wrote a figure: $2 million. The following Monday I accepted the offer, and within two weeks I was moving my family across California on nothing more than a promise. It ultimately worked out and after I sold that company, I had the bug. I wanted to do it again and again and I have—almost all my ventures have been in healthcare and technology and the supply chain. Once I get my current company, Z5 Inventory, as big as I can possibly make it, I'll probably go out and find another small idea that I can help to make big.

What challenges have you faced?

The first company I started eventually received a $20 million term sheet from SoftBank—the biggest investor in tech companies in the world—that valued us at $100 million. I was having a dinner party with a bunch of friends at my house to celebrate. The market crashed that day. During dinner, the SoftBank partner called and told me they were pulling the term sheet. That, coupled with the crash, forced me to reduce my staff from 40 to 10. That was incredibly hard. But we reevaluated what we wanted to offer as a company and ultimately we came out stronger for it.

What have you learned?

1. It takes a long time to implement change in healthcare. These are long, long change cycles. We have a prominent client who's just coming around to the idea of Z5 Inventory, and we first approached them almost five years ago. That's how long it takes to convince the industry that a solution is to their benefit.

2. It's more challenging to raise capital for a less glitzy solution. Inventory management isn't a sexy idea. It's not creating a social media network or giving everybody electric scooters! Investors are looking for something with a bit more glamour. So we have to work harder to shock them with our value proposition.

3. Manufacturing works against anything it sees as a threat. The makers and distributors of medical supplies have actively worked to undermine our kind of progress because the status quo benefits them. These companies have a lot of resources—boots on the ground and voices in the ear—but we've got enough determination to show them the old ways of doing business can't last.

4. Always have a mindset of "how can that be done better?" If you're looking for ways to improve you'll

discover micro-benefits, like a way to get more time to yourself in the day, and macro-benefits, like the next big idea that might change the world.

5. You'll never wish you were more of a bastard. Treat everyone you encounter with respect, and they'll respect you and your business. Even more than respect, compassion goes a long way.

Follow on Twitter: @Z5Inventory

HEALTHCARE IN THE COMMUNITY

Ruth Williams-Brinkley

PRESIDENT, KAISER FOUNDATION HEALTH PLAN AND HOSPITALS OF THE NORTHWEST

The intersection of community and health is perhaps one of the biggest opportunities and challenges we face in healthcare. We know that healthcare services account for less than 20 percent of what determines a person's health status. Most healthcare happens outside the doctor's office—in the communities where people live, work, and play.

As healthcare providers, we need to look beyond the walls of our facilities and broaden the definition of what it means to provide care. At Kaiser Permanente, we're making tangible contributions to build up the communities we serve by investing in areas like food insecurity, housing, gun safety, and mental health and wellness services. We're also reaching out to our community health partners to strengthen safety nets to support our patients when they are out of our clinics.

Leading the transformation of health and healthcare in the United States requires us to think and act in new ways, reimagining what is possible.

Q&A WITH RUTH WILLIAMS-BRINKLEY

What brought you to this career?

I always say that I didn't choose healthcare... it chose me. When I went to college, I wasn't quite sure what I wanted to be. My grandmother encouraged me to explore a career as a nurse—something I initially rebelled against. But in the end, my grandmother knew best. After graduating, I started my healthcare career as a post-anesthesia nurse in Chicago. Today, as a healthcare CEO, I keep my training and experience as a nurse top of mind as I make decisions that affect the health and lives of our members and employees.

What really recommitted me to healthcare was the loss of a family member, who was misdiagnosed and eventually passed away in a hospital. I spent countless hours in that hospital and saw the best of our healthcare system. But most of all, I saw people dedicated to caring for my family member—and me. During that intense time, things came full circle for me. Ultimately, it was a nurse who was the angel that I needed. She was compassionate, honest, and truthful without taking away hope.

What do you believe in?

I believe that we are on a mission in life to help others. Personally, I'm focused on building others up at all levels—whether it's mentoring the next generation of healthcare workers or fostering diversity and inclusion at the highest leadership levels in large organizations. I've worked in healthcare for my entire career and it's a stressful field. That's why I'm also very aware of the importance of finding something that brings joy to balance out the hard work we all do.

Follow on LinkedIn:
https://www.linkedin.com/in/ruthwilliamsbrinkley/

A New Way of Thinking about Dying

Dr. Tim Ihrig

CHIEF MEDICAL OFFICER, CROSSROADS HOSPICE AND FOUNDER AND CEO, IHRIG MD & ASSOCIATES

Harold was my very first patient. It was my first day with the long white coat and I was the on-call resident at a Veterans Administration hospital. Harold was in his late sixties and came to the emergency department with a primary complaint of headaches that had been getting worse and worse over the past month or so. A CT scan revealed that he had widely metastatic cancer. It had spread throughout his body, including his brain—thus the headaches. The attending physician instructed me to share with Harold and his family the findings, prognosis and options for care. While we didn't know the type of cancer, this was a moot point—people do not recover from such extensive disease.

As I was only a few hours into my career as a physician, I did the only thing I was absolutely sure of. I walked into Harold's room, sat down, took his hand, took his wife's hand and just breathed. After a few moments he said, "It's not good news is it, sonny?"

I said, "No."

And so we talked and we listened and we shared. After a bit, I asked what it was that brought meaning to Harold. I asked, "What is it that you hold sacred?"

He replied, "My family." He had a wife and two teenage daughters.

I asked what he would like to do. He slapped me on the knee and said, "I'd like to go fishing."

I said, "That, I know how to do." He went fishing the next day. He died a week later.

Harold exemplifies the tremendous opportunity we have to connect to a broader sense of the human condition beyond ourselves. The key and challenge is moving beyond the linear algorithmic model of healthcare, by which things are done to you because you have X, Y or Z. This approach does not parallel the algorithm of life—especially when it comes to the seriously ill. This linear algorithm is static. But the seriously ill need a flexible, dynamic model—one which mimics the algorithm of life.

The key is to be accepting of the true algorithm of life—the variability of the day-to-day within the context of knowing exactly what is ultimately going to happen [death] regardless of ailment or intervention. It's even more important to realize and accept that we can't overcome it—we can't beat Mother Nature. I whole-heartedly support "fighting" and "never giving up" but we first need to define exactly what we are "fighting for". We need to align clinical endeavors (aggressive or not) with the realities of the human physiologic trajectory and, as always, what is sacred to the individual.

Harold inspired me to strive to care for people based on what is sacred to them, regardless of diagnosis or age. I have focused on doing things with and for people, rather than doing things to them. I have rejected healthcare's existing transactional relationship in favor of a translational relationship—one where the patient is the true center of care.

We need to put the "care" back in healthcare. We need to be willing to truly engage with our patients and make sure their treatment program is a shared decision and a shared journey between practitioner and patient. We need to hold classmates, colleagues, and ourselves accountable for our actions, beliefs and behaviors. We need to be a catalyst of truth. We need to be a new voice in healthcare so patients can find their own. We need to care.

My "big idea" is to start a revolution of thought which brings forth a shift in our understanding of life and how we practice medicine. We must deconstruct the current model of healthcare as it unequivocally lacks the ability to care for the most ill, vulnerable and dying people on the planet. In addition, it jeopardizes not only the global economy, but, more importantly, our own humanity. We need to go beyond historic ways of thinking to solve these problems. As a colleague once said, "The electric light was not invented through the improvement of candles."

A revolution provides the opportunity to change the paradigm of medical practice by acting as both the philosophy predicating the deconstruction of this inadequate healthcare model and the architecture of a new system—one that meets current and future needs in a truly person-centric and economically viable model. Too often when people hear the term palliative care, they associate it with dying. In reality, it's about living based on our values, what we find sacred, and how we want to write the chapters of our lives—whether it's the last chapter or the last five.

I remember a 105-year old woman who was brought to the hospital by her family—four generations of them! She had shortness of breath, an irregular heart rhythm and swelling in her legs. She was dying from being old, not because there was anything wrong with her that could be fixed. Her heart—her whole body— was physiologically worn out. A cardiology colleague recommended a cardiac catheterization, possible pacemaker implantation and various pharmacologic interventions. The patient very politely said, "No thank you. I'd like to go home."

I urge us to seek new ways of thinking and practicing medicine which elevate what is possible in healthcare and beyond. Deepening our understanding of life, as opposed to fearing death or thinking of it as the ultimate clinical failure, we transcend medicine and come closer to what it means to be a true caregiver in the modern age.

Q&A WITH TIM IHRIG

What have you learned in your career?

The healthcare system is misaligned with respect to true patient-centricity. One experience stands out. Early in my career, the chief medical officer (CMO) of the healthcare system I worked in called me to his office. He told me how frustrated and angry many of the oncologists were that I offered clinical opinions to cancer patients when they asked about their prognosis and disease states. Many of these individuals, like Harold, had incurable cancers that were going to kill them. A majority of these people had never been told this truth. They were, literally and figuratively, dying while continuing to receive horrifically aggressive chemotherapeutic interventions at the insistence of their doctors. When empowered with the truth, many sought more honest engagements with these doctors and questioned the efficacy of continuing such treatments if they weren't going to make any positive difference in the quality or length of their lives.

Follow on Twitter: @IhrigMD

Healthcare Environment

Medical management like clinical decision support tools, physician training, big data (preparation, insights)

If we look at the patient journey as an island, the healthcare environment is the ocean around it. It is the ecosystem that we all live in, and the sometimes-confusing maze that we navigate in.

In this chapter, we will explore the different areas of the healthcare environment—from entrepreneurship to venture capitalists, career management, and the role of technology.

Directly from seasoned and experienced executives, you will gain the best roadmap on how to navigate the various landscapes of healthcare.

"Were there none who were discontented with what they have, the world would never reach anything better."

—Florence Nightingale

IT INFRASTRUCTURE FOR HEALTHCARE

Barbara W. Casey

GLOBAL HEALTHCARE LEADER, CISCO SYSTEMS, INC.

Cisco is unique in the world of digital health as it is truly alone—there is no other competitor that has the same elements within its technology portfolio. We may have competition in a single architecture—enterprise networking, data center, security or collaboration—but no one else has all of these in combination. So, when we're striving for connected health, there is no other organization capable of delivering what Cisco can in terms of core infrastructure and platform capabilities, that can be built on to achieve amazing things.

There are many stories where this becomes important. One is where the "whole IT stack" is not considered and so expectations are not met. Let's say a service-line leader (e.g. neurology), physician and team selects a point solution for telestroke [stroke telemedicine]. They do an RFP (request for proposal), they conduct a thorough search and they choose an application with many bells and whistles. As they implement, they see it's not quite working the way they envisioned, and not even as well as it did in the demos. It's slow, has poor video quality, it times out or it abruptly stops in the middle of a session. The mainly-clinical team who conducted the selection process is disappointed in the results and wonders why, but blames the application vendor.

If they were to do a root-cause analysis, they would discover that maybe the application was working just fine, but that their network was to blame, or the way the video was configured to run in their existing collaboration environment was not quite optimal. These types of digital solutions require a deep understanding of multiple technology domains to run effectively. In this example, Cisco has solutions and expertise to bring all of these domains to the table and to ensure they are working optimally to achieve the desired outcome.

One of the most exciting projects our team is working on is with HIMSS Analytics around their INFRAM—Infrastructure Adoption Model.[8] This project represents a collaboration between HIMSS Analytics and Cisco and the goal is to help healthcare organizations understand what levels of infrastructure they need in order to achieve higher-order business or clinical capabilities. Unless the right networking, security or data center solution and architecture is in place, the clinical and business applications or solutions will not perform as intended. Therefore, the INFRAM helps to create that linkage between infrastructure and clinical/business operations performance and raise awareness among the respective leaders that you cannot have one without the other.

Q&A with Barbara W. Casey

How can we improve the healthcare system?

1. Establish a personal health record (PHR) for each person in the United States. If every person had a PHR, each person would own their own data and then decide how it gets shared, mined, used, etc. Microsoft HealthVault and Google Health maybe were ahead of their time when they introduced these concepts.

2. Institute a basic level of health insurance coverage for all US citizens. Health insurance at a basic level should be affordable and available to all. Obamacare probably got us the closest but it's mostly been walked back. I believe each person should have preventative services covered (screenings, immunizations, basic diagnostics to gauge their current state of health, and other types of primary care) and probably catastrophic insurance for trauma or emergencies.

3. Drive the right alternative reimbursement models to gain more care coordination and accountability. Move beyond FFS (fee-for-service) payment, drive the

concept of the patient-centered medical home (PCMH) and put accountability on whole-provider systems or networks to manage dollars per patient across the continuum of care.

4. Create digital health capabilities for consumers that are at least on par with other industries. Consumers/patients should be able to email or text their providers, make appointments online, compare prices for common procedures or tests, get prescription refills or lab results online, see clinicians remotely via video or phone, and get prescriptions delivered to their home. Excellent consumer service should be a goal for a physician practice. Right now, they are still closed for lunch (even to phone calls) and on Fridays—that's the "dark ages" for service.

5. If chronically ill and elderly patients are consuming the most healthcare resources, we need to provide greater support for this population. People don't have to be nurses or doctors to provide outreach to those in need. They can be relatively inexpensive, but well-trained, individuals. For example, someone to make sure that the environment is safe from fall hazards, someone to understand the food and nutrition situation and needs, and someone to assess the person's mental state and how isolated the person is socially.

What steps should we take to improve the system?

Individuals should demand to be treated differently by healthcare providers! Review your physician practices, surgery centers and hospitals online. Treat them as any other consumer business and provide feedback constructively about how you expect to be treated and communicated with.

Corporations should create future-state strategies by envisioning what is possible, then create the organizational structure to make it happen. This is a big barrier in healthcare organizations today. They have no leader or function that oversees the consumer/patient/family experience across the continuum of care, even though they may own 80 percent of it!

There needs to be a chief digitization officer who wakes up every morning thinking of how the customer journey unfolds from the doctor's office to the diagnostic/imaging center, to the ASC (ambulatory surgery center), to the hospital, and across post-acute care, back into the home. Are all those experiences seamless? Is it easy for the consumer/patient/family to consume care in and across these settings?

And when people are billed for services, does it make sense? Has everything been done to coordinate these motions so that it's as easy as possible for the consumer/patient/family to do business with the corporation as the provider or payer? These are first-order operational/clinical/financial goals that any corporation should apply to healthcare today.

In communities, it's all about outreach. When I was building Medicaid plans in Detroit or Arizona, we did a tremendous amount of research to understand the population and their culture. Where did they hang out? Where did they spend social time? What were their lives like? Once we understood these factors, we then created logical "moments that matter" in terms of outreach or education in places where they already were. In Detroit, we put Medicaid enrollment centers in churches, barber shops, and WIC (Women, Infants and Children) clinics. We did screenings and flu shots at county fairs and other highly frequented sites in the community. Education sessions were done in public schools, starting in elementary grades, about the important of nutrition and mental health, as well as primary care. Working across several public-sector groups and like-minded community programs with an aligned goal of a healthier population is key.

Follow on Twitter: @barbarawcasey
Blog: https://blogs.cisco.com/author/barbaracasey

INTEGRATION OF INSURANCE PAYERS, PROVIDERS, AND PATIENTS

Rushil Desai

VICE PRESIDENT, PROVIDER STRATEGY AND PERFORMANCE OUTCOMES, ILLINICARE HEALTH

IlliniCare Health is a managed care organization in Illinois. In my current role, I get to tackle some fun questions. Where are the opportunities for us to grow strategically? How do we work better with our providers? And how do we use analytics and data and the capabilities of our plan to help providers?

We are changing the previous payer-provider relationship dynamic. Rather than payers and providers acting from opposite ends of the table, we are identifying synergies to bridge that gap, and looking to find new dynamics and playing fields for looking at the goal as a team. Data is the currency in our realm right now. As we grow as an industry and an organization, data will become essential in how we progress. I believe the transparency of data is key to how we have been successful in working with our providers. That free flow of information between providers and payers leads to building centers of excellence. We provide transparency, from finances to the regimen to expense and the predictive side of things.

Right now, we are focused heavily on predictive analytics and machine learning in population health. For example, out of a 400,000 member population, we know that roughly 5 percent of that population will drive 50 percent of the overall expenses. So with that data, we focus on the most acute membership, the members that we are unable to reach and the ones that providers need to be aware of. Together, the goals of providers and payers are aligned, trust is built, and we build an integrated system. And key to creating that system is the transparent sharing of data and analytics.

A potential drawback is that, as an industry, we still do not have a complete picture and it's very segmented. Payers work off of claims data, which has a lag. Providers work off of EMR access. Right now, we do not have the two sources of data integration, and because it is not cohesive, we do not yet have a complete grasp of the full picture of the member. Although there is a lot of new technology coming out to help solve this problem, such as the Apple Watch, that provide personalized health and digital health, the integration between payers, providers and patients is still a challenge.

It's going to take a bit of time for us to get to that perfect integration, where the data cycle from patient to provider to the payer is collected in one place. We are just scratching the surface, and we're not quite there yet.

Q&A WITH RUSHIL DESAI

What brought you to this career?

At Miami, I majored in neuroscience at the University of Miami. Shortly after, I obtained my master's in Biomedical Science and Healthcare Administration at Rosalind Franklin University's Chicago Medical School. A year after that, I attended medical school for three years. In my third year, I became heavily involved with the leadership side of the school but I started experiencing burnout and wasn't sure if I still wanted to be a physician.

I ended up taking some time off, worked at the University of Chicago Hospital, and attended Duke University's Fuqua School of Business. During my MBA, I was the senior principal and healthcare lead of Improving Health & Outcomes at Trexin Consulting. There, I gained exposure to a variety of payers and providers, as well as the challenges that healthcare is facing. They included managing the cost of care, large-scale transformation, moving towards value-based care, and clinical program redesign, from strategy to execution.

Looking back, it was essential to have that consulting experience and to be able to focus on different techniques to manage the cost of care and integrate the financial side of healthcare with the clinical side. We tackled questions such as how do providers and payers collaborate? And where are the opportunities to address the social determinants of health to focus on the most acute patients through population health analytics?

What do you look for when you're hiring?

I like to hire people who may not have a healthcare education or background. People can learn the healthcare side, but bringing out the strength to move teams toward a common purpose leads to success. But people who come from outside industries bring valuable diversity and thought. In my current team, I have folks with backgrounds in analytical knowledge, learning skills, and finance strategy.

How can we future-proof our careers?

We are experiencing a lot of mergers and acquisitions. We are mixing insurers with pharmacy benefit managers, and we see hospitals mixing with payers. I think the reason why the healthcare industry is changing so much daily is that we haven't quite figured out the best mix yet. So it's critical to have an open mind, have data competencies, and never lose empathy for members or patients. Strong interpersonal skills and diverse perspectives and problem solving is key. Outside of your team, it's vital to surround yourself with people who constantly challenge you, push you and help you grow. I think that solutions in healthcare are integrated so you have to learn all the different elements, from contracting to networking, quality, medical management and finance.

Follow on Twitter: @IlliniCare

DEMOCRATIZING VISION IN THE DEVELOPING WORLD

Jordan Kassalow

FOUNDER, VISIONSPRING AND EYELLIANCE

Around the world, 2.5 billion people suffer from poor vision. That's not because of an eye disease, but just because they need a pair of glasses to see optimally. At VisionSpring, our big idea is to radically scale our ability to provide affordable and high-quality eye care and eye-care products to underserved people throughout the world.

Vision is incredibly important to human potential and human capital. Because 80% of our sensory input comes through our eyes, it is critical to learning, productivity, livelihoods, and safety. Children with poor vision often fall out of school, and adults with poor vision often fall out of the workforce. And one of the leading causes of death in the developing world is road traffic accidents, 59% of which have a visual component associated with them.

From my travels in Latin America and later India and Africa, I observed that the biggest need for glasses was among the 40-something-year-old individuals who had started to lose their close-up vision. Many of these people were earning their living with their eyes and hands—they were weavers, tailors, artisans, and mechanics. If you took them out of the workforce because they could no longer see, it had a very detrimental impact on them, their families, and their communities.

The proverbial lightbulb moment came when I was traveling throughout central and west Africa. I was providing medicine for people suffering from "river blindness" disease. Wherever I visited, I asked people what they needed most. The answers were obvious things like better healthcare, education and clean water, but a woman farmer in central Cameroon said "we really only need one thing, and that is opportunity. If we have opportunity, we can be self-reliant: we can have education, we can have healthcare, and we can have clean water." That really stopped me in my tracks and I made the connection between glasses and opportunity.

This is one of the stories I share in my book *Dare To Matter: Your Path to Making a Difference Now*, co-written with Jennifer Krause. The book is about living a life that honors two fundamental human needs: to take care of yourself and your family and to live a life that takes care of others. One of the most powerful stories in the book is about a woman named Noka, who I met in Colombia. She was known in her village as the blind lady, and she spent a full day in a canoe to come to our clinic. And sure enough, she couldn't see at all. But the good news was that her vision was entirely correctable with a very strong pair of glasses. We put the glasses on her face and she was able to see for the first time in her life.

Three days later, she returns with complaints that the people in her village laughed at her and ostracized her because her glasses looked so funny. And she was right—the glasses were 1950s cat eyeglasses with rhinestones. We explained that these were the only pair we had available in her prescription. When she heard that, she did something that shocked us. She took her glasses off, left them behind, and went up the river blind. When someone chooses blindness over your solution, you need to do something about it. This is an example of putting the problem in front of the person.

What we realized was that there can be a lot of cultural nuances. When I first started, I thought selling glasses was going to be a piece of cake and that they would fly off the shelf like cell phones. But in India, girls of marriageable age thought they were less marriageable if they had glasses. And in Cambodia, Pol Pot killed many intellectuals and there are images of giant mounds of glasses collected from the executed. In their minds, wearing glasses can equate to being killed. We've learned to understand these cultural biases as well regulatory challenges, the supply chain, and the entire system that we are trying to address.

Everywhere I went, I observed that there were a lot of underemployed people, particularly women. The original idea was to focus on simple reading glasses, and to see if we could train local women to screen for vision impairment and sell simple glasses to their neighbors. That way, the women would have an opportunity to get new jobs, and people who buy the glasses could sustain their career. We started out with 18 women in India and sold over 800 pairs of glasses in our first year. Fast forward to now and we have over 30,000 women worldwide. Between them and our other business units, we sold close to 1.2 million pairs of glasses in 2018. If we can democratize vision and bridge the gap between those who have it and those who don't, we can change the world.

Q&A WITH JORDAN KASSALOW

What brought you to this career?

As a first-year student at optometry school, I joined an organization that brought eye care to underserved populations in Mexico. My first patient was a seven-year-old boy named Raul, who had grown up believing he was blind. But when I looked into his eyes, I realized he wasn't. He just needed a very strong pair of eyeglasses. I was the person who put glasses on his face for the first time. You can imagine how fundamentally it changed his life as well as mind—when he saw clearly for the first time. So I started on this career path of trying to help people see so that they can live to their full potential. I've since been named in the *Forbes* Impact 30 and was the inaugural winner of the John P. McNulty Prize.

Are there any potential drawbacks?

There are unintended consequences. What if we'd provided Raul with glasses and then in a year's time, he'd lost or broken them? If we hadn't created a way for him to get his future glasses, did we really do him a favor? So, the unintended consequences is that once we provide people with their first vision, we are obligated to provide them with their second and third pair, and to create a sustainable supply chain.

What have you learned?

It's all about partnerships: you've got to partner wisely. When we first started VisionSpring, we were trying to do everything on our own. We identified women entrepreneurs, trained them, managed them, supplied them with glasses. Then we discovered an organization in Bangladesh called BRAC. It already had an incredible network of community health workers selling products. All we would need to do was train them how to screen for vision problems and sell reading glasses. And we did. Through our partnerships, our numbers and scale just took off. As well as partnerships, it's really helpful to be mentored by people who are 10 or 30 years older than you, as well as people younger than you who have new and fresh perspectives.

What do you believe in?

Practice dying—this is core to what we do. It's the realization that we are not going to be around forever—we don't really know how long we are going to be here. There's an urgency to living a life that has meaning. A key goal of *Dare to Matter* is helping people realize earlier what really matters in life so that they have more time to do something of significance with that knowledge. Also, practice gratitude. Feel grateful to those who are making your life richer or helping your vision or big idea come to life.

Follow on Twitter: @visionspring

HOW TO FIND INVESTORS FOR YOUR STARTUP

Judy Robinett

AUTHOR, *CRACK THE FUNDING CODE: HOW INVESTORS THINK AND WHAT THEY NEED TO HEAR TO FUND YOUR STARTUP* AND *HOW TO BE A POWER CONNECTOR: THE 5-50-150 RULE*

I've met many terrific entrepreneurs around the world who couldn't figure out how to find an investor. So having been an investor, I decided I could demystify that world a little. One of the fundamental principles of my book *Crack the Funding Code* is that there is no lack of money. Credit Suisse's Annual Wealth Report for 2018 found that there was $317 trillion of global wealth, and there are more than 300 angel groups in the United States. We now have private offices for wealthy families who are seeing more deals than VCs [venture capitalists].

One section of my book focuses on who those investors are and where you can find them. And they are everywhere! You can google "find local investors" or you can reach out to the local SBA [Small Business Administration], the SBDC [Small Business

Development Center], Score, or your university entrepreneur programs. I had one VC tell me, "If you can't figure out how to get to me, you can't figure out how to get a customer." Talk to lawyers, bankers and accountants that work with startups. Other entrepreneurs can be incredibly valuable too.

Another fundamental principle in my book centers on the founder's mistakes. Many founders make the mistake of thinking "look how cool my idea is! Don't you want to drink my Kool-Aid?" Instead, investors are wondering how they are going to get their money back and if it is a viable business. That's why it's important to set yourself apart as a high-potential startup. To do this, you need to package your business well. First, be clear on your exit strategy.

Second, mitigate risks as viewed by the investor. Investors are investing in you as the founder; and they want to know that you can execute and your team can perform. You are risking the investor's money. They want to know that the dog will eat the dog food. Will customers open their wallets and pay for this thing you've created? What is the size of the market? Is it big enough for them to get a good return on their investment? Do you have traction? One way to mitigate these risks is to form an advisory board and recruit key advisors. If you are a first-time founder, bring in people with gravitas to add credibility. It's also wise to listen to them as they have done it before.

A third principle in my book is the three Cs. As a founder, you must be coachable, you must have good character, and you must have confidence. A sure way to kill your deal is to come across as a know-it-all or to be untruthful. Investors will run, not walk, away from your deal. It's important to understand the mindset of an investor, understand where those investors are and the different types, and to understand how to package your deal. It's always important to find the appropriate angels and VCs. You still need a compelling story and a great pitch deck, but it is critical to build relationships and find the right investment groups before you ask for money.

I've always known that there is no lack of creativity or innovation in the world. We should have more entrepreneurs. I wrote my book because it hurt my heart that people couldn't get funded when they have something that could change the world. Clayton Christensen's book, *The Prosperity Paradox*, is about the fact that many third-world countries are now worse off than before they were given $6.4 trillion in aid to improve lives and create jobs. Clayton discovered that the way to change the world is to have entrepreneurs who create markets. Change must come from the bottom up, not the top down.

Q&A with Judy Robinett

What brought you to this career?

While I was working for a Fortune 100 company, I was handed a *Wall Street Journal* article highlighting five ways to become financially independent in America. They were: be a lawyer, a doctor, inherit, marry into it or start a business. I thought, "Start a business! How hard can it be?" So I acquired a couple of partners and secured a $1.3 million SBA loan to build a franchise restaurant. Several years later, I thought I was going to lose everything because I was broke. I went to a bankruptcy attorney who looked at my financials and said, "They can break you, but they can't eat you." That cured me of my fear. I turned the franchise around and sold it.

I discovered that many companies needed help to turn around, from failing to succeeding. It was the same story, the same play, but with different actors. I was asked to help with a public biotech company and was the CEO for 10 years. Then I was asked to evaluate an unknown startup, Skullcandy, for an investor. It went public in 2011 for just under half a billion dollars. Then I became fascinated with startups and their power to change the world. I became an investor and now sit on VC boards. I'm an advisor to Springboard,[9] an incubator that works exclusively with women founders.

Companies completing the program have raised over $7 billion, had 19 IPOs and 180 strategic sales.

What do investors look for in healthcare startups?

One of my favorite angel groups is Life Science Angels[10] in San Francisco, which focuses exclusively on life sciences—typically diagnostics and medical devices, and not as much on pharma and drug discovery. There are now more than 60 venture capital firms looking at life sciences because it is one of the industries with the highest returns. In 2018, VCs invested over $28.8 billion. Besides VC funding, we have sovereign wealth funds with $8 trillion, 6,000 family offices with $4 trillion, corporate VCs and more than 400 angel groups who all syndicate with each other. There are also large family offices which are investing in healthcare.

What have you learned?

I wish I had known that most people will help you if you ask. I should have learned the skill of asking a lot earlier. Also, I wish I had learned to talk to strangers earlier because that's where the gold is! I've met billionaires hiking in Park City. I wish I had discovered earlier what I call my three golden questions. Everybody's problem is somebody else's solution. The problem that entrepreneurs have is finding money. The problem that investors have is finding a great deal, and they are willing to give up money to get that deal. My number one golden question is "how can I help?" The second question to ask, after you share what you are doing, is "what other ideas do you have for me?" The third question is "who else do you know who I should talk to?" These questions have helped me land opportunities to visit the White House for fintech conferences, serve on panels with Mark Cuban and go on Fox Business Mornings with Maria Bartiromo. I would never have guessed in a hundred years that I would be able to do any of that.

Follow on Twitter: @judyrobinett

Shaden Marzouk
MD, MBA

MANAGING DIRECTOR, HEALTH, AXA

What brought you to this career?

When I was in medical school, I chose neurosurgery as my specialty because of the challenge it provided. That was also the reason I picked my sub-specialty in spine surgery. I did a fellowship in adult deformity and was very interested in the biomechanics and helping people with their spine problems, as well as the challenges that spine problems pose. I am a neurosurgeon and I spent a significant portion of my life doing neurosurgery, seeing patients in clinic, operating rooms, and hospitals, as well as conducting clinical research. I did a career transition from the patient side to the business side of healthcare by getting my MBA at the Fuqua School of Business at Duke University. That was a wonderful decision. Post-MBA, I worked at Goldman Sachs as an associate in the investment bank, then moved to one of my clients, Cardinal Health. I was at Cardinal Health for six and a half years in a succession of roles. The reason that I moved to the business side was because I was looking for a platform that was larger than one patient at a time to address the issues we see in our healthcare system today.

What are you most excited about in your industry?

I am very excited about the innovation that seems to be coming through on the technology side, and on the service side. There is a greater understanding that patients are consumers and that healthcare can change. More and more, we have the tools to do that. I've been particularly interested in telemedicine and the delivery of virtual care. I'm also interested in remote monitoring and all that we can do with wearables and peripherals, as well as apps that drive patient adherence and engagement. Technology and tech-enabled solutions that help decrease cost, highlight quality, and increase access are exciting (and needed).

What principles have guided you?

I've taken risks in my life and with risk comes reward. I took a risk going to neurosurgery. It was a very hard specialty to get into, and I felt very rewarded by the profession. I took another risk in changing my career a little later in life to the business side of healthcare. For me, that was the right decision. If I did things again, I would do them the same way. I'm often asked to mentor people, and I advise them to take risks. Risk-taking can end up in a negative scenario but it can also end up in a positive scenario, and you'll learn from both. In addition, healthcare is global as regards the challenges that patients and providers face. I think it is very important to have global experiences in your career.

What advice would you give others?

1. Get the right education. In my current role, it's very helpful that I'm a doctor. It's a commitment that you make, but it's given me quite a bit of useful knowledge and experience. Moving over to the business side of healthcare was enabled tremendously by my experience at the Fuqua School of Business at Duke University, particularly by the knowledge, the network and the mentoring that I gained at Fuqua.

2. Take risks. There are a lot of great things that happen in life when you try to do something where failure is a potential outcome, but then you keep going and think about how to continue to solve the challenges in front of you.

3. Always communicate and present things concisely, confidently and clearly.

Jeff Elkins

Chief Operating Officer, InterVene Medical

I enjoy watching the emergence of large-scale fields. I've been lucky to have had a front-row seat to watch emerging markets relating to the heart, brain and peripheral arteries—emerging fields that started from nothing. I often see very out-of-the-box ideas, often from physicians, but I don't get scared off by something that may not exist. I'm very willing to see if it might emerge in the next 10–20 years.

In the early days, I was involved in aortic endografting, which is a conversion from a very invasive, very high-risk open surgery. Aortic endografting started in the early 1990s, and I got involved in 1997. A small group of physicians were willing to try this high risk, minimally invasive approach. It's high risk because if or when things go wrong, you have to open up the patients and do surgery.

It was a really interesting time because half the world said that it would never work and the other half said it would. There were tons of very hairy procedures, and some tough failures that required you to keep on going. Now, this is a $1.3–1.7 billion market worldwide. It' s very mature and established as a standard of care. But back in 1997–1998, it was just getting going and we didn't know if it was going to make it or not.

When pitching to investors, start with the background, including the experience and pedigree of your team, because it helps establish your credibility. It's also important to try to make your pitch concise. Boil down the most important message in a very digestible, visually appealing, well-produced way. That includes the look, the layout, and the format. You have to be confident— you can't be hesitant about answers or the probability of success. You also can't just focus on one thing, such as tech, without thinking of the regulatory aspects or timelines. You have to focus on all things and have a comprehensive overview of business—its risks, upsides, competitors, patients, and financials, and have a real handle on your entire business and plan.

I put a huge premium on anticipating the questions that will come up from investors. You should anticipate all the questions from the various partners of the firm. Expect commercial questions, statistics, regulatory paths, and competitive questions. I will go in with answers for 1,000 questions, but you only need 100. But you don't know which 100, so you need to be ready.

Never come to a pitch dreaming of a lucrative and quick exit. Be positive and paint a good picture, but stay grounded and realistic.

One way I stand out with investors is to prepare so that I know a little more than normal about my technology. I've been in the operating rooms and I can quote scientific literature and the history behind it. I can understand how something developed—the economics, reimbursements, engineering, and margins. I try to have a strong command of my materials and the area that I'm working in.

Q&A WITH JEFF ELKINS

What advice would you give others?

1. Take calculated risks

It's important to jump into opportunities and get out of your comfort zone. If you are an engineer, engage with customers or switch to finances, business development or marketing. Leaving that comfort zone is very important. Don't just ask "can something be done?" but look at what is necessary in terms of resources, time and money. I constantly look out for landmines too. I think about project spending, the team and the timing and consider the landmines that will kill the project or cause a delay. I put a lot of time into risk management, looking for places that are going to fail and then create the means to mitigate it and screen out the risks as much as possible.

2. Take an unconventional approach

There is a lot to be said for unconventional approaches. If you get stuck in an established pattern of thinking, it's limiting. You have to be willing to think outside of that paradigm. For this reason, surround yourself with multi-position players. I put a lot of value on people who can do multiple roles—people with multiple perspectives. For example, someone with field perspective who designs a project, someone who writes regulatory documents because they understand both the risks and clinical patients. Or engineers with marketing experience.

3. Work hard

Do whatever it takes. Whatever crazy hours, travel, and out-of-box solutions it takes to get it done, you need to do it because in the startup world, it is really hard to get an exit. At all times, give very high quality of work. If you are expected to deliver something, exceed it, whether that's in terms of quality or timeliness or completeness. And try harder whatever you are doing. Whether you are competing with a company or with another person, put in more effort, more thought, and more worry so that you simply do a better job.

Whatever field I'm in, I am completely immersed and try to understand everything about it—the science, the history, who the thought leaders are, society, standards of care—so that I can be a first-hand expert. I may not be a statistical guru or CFO, but I have to understand it enough to converse on all levels.

4. Handle adversity

In the startup world, failures are normal. I go into it understanding that it will be like a rollercoaster ride. Facing adversity and failure just comes with the territory. Know that failure will happen and have everyone ready when it does. In our world, examples can be running out of money, having difficulty raising funds, or a patient who dies or gets injured with your product. There are also FDA delays and regulatory approval costs. It could be a competitor with a big victory, or the devices you are using to train physicians not showing up on time. At minimum, you have to plan for it, assume that these emergencies happen, and teach everyone it's normal. I'm always comfortable taking big risks if the worst case is that the company goes out of business. But I never take unreasonable risks on patients or patient safety.

Conclusion

As we peek into this crystal ball, we are given a once-in-a-lifetime view of what the future might hold, of the innovations ahead.

The future of healthcare will see an influx of early disease-detection methods. We will see these techniques shared and applied to a variety of industries outside of healthcare.

We will see the evolution of gene-editing technologies, and witness the partial and complete eradication of diseases. Our children may grow up in a world where cancer and dementia are a thing of the past.

We will marvel at the awesome power of the Internet of Things, unleashed by 5G connectivity. We will feast our eyes on how artificial intelligence and machine learning streamline drug research and discovery, preventing waste and lowering costs.

And we will be amazed at the creative solutions centered on the adoption of robots and virtual-reality simulations.

However, if you take one thing with you from this book, it's this:

Frustration with the status quo is good. If you know what it is that causes you frustration, if you keep a sharp eye on industry dynamics, if you allow failure in your life, then you can build that next big thing that will completely, utterly, and totally change our world.

Sickness, pain, and terrible, horrible, no-good experiences can be the catalyst to breaking what doesn't work and rebuilding it with something better. A loved one's diagnosis, a mistreatment of a stranger, a terrible it-happened-to-me story can lead to the creation of something so much greater than yourself, so much greater than any of us can imagine.

The innovator's philosophy

Your venture, your creation, your legacy can be all-encompassing. It can be your entire world. But it shouldn't be. Make sure to balance your work with a firm, unshakeable foundation of values and beliefs.

Our innovators share common philosophies. First and foremost, question everything. Read avidly. Learn, and don't take conventional wisdom as the truth. Identify the one or two activities with the greatest impact, and focus on these activities. Hire the best people, trust them, and get out of their way. Be okay with failure. Be a bit "irrational." Take bets and try things that others have shied away from. Take those painful, terrible, excruciating experiences and turn them into something better, something bigger than yourself. Do the right thing because it is the right thing, not because someone is looking.

Future-proofing you

All of our innovators agree on one thing. The future of work is unclear. We don't know how it will play out. The only constant is change. So, knowing that—

- Be adept at embracing new ideas, and evolve your skills. Have a wide range of proficiencies. It will make you harder to replace for your employer, and harder for a machine to take over your position.

- Know the difference between "I don't know how to do that." and "I don't want to take the time to figure that out."

- Even if it is difficult, even if you are afraid, embrace and utilize technology. Learn to incorporate it into your work. Keep your eyes open for moments that could create new pathways and new opportunities. Monetize the skills you do have and look to generate income from a side venture.

Finally, if what you are doing is in service to humanity, if it—in some way—contributes to the greater good, then you are already paving the way to a future-proof career.

So, go out there and find that thing that doesn't work. Identify that tension point. Tackle that Big Hairy Complicated Problem. Pick up your armor, saddle your horse, and prepare to fight, to build, to innovate.

For, as a wise man once asked, "If not us, then who? And, if not now, then when?"

Notes

1. https://www.thelancet.com/journals/lancet/article/PIIS0140-6736%2813%2961249-0/fulltext

2. https://evtoday.com/2011/08/the-costs-of-critical-limb-ischemia

3. https://www.sciencedirect.com/science/article/pii/S1078588413002256

4. https://www.axobio.com/leadership-3

5. https://www.telehealth.va.gov/

6. https://www.bfrb.org

7. https://www.ajicjournal.org/article/S0196-6553%2818%2930948-9/fulltext

8. https://www.himssanalytics.org/infram

9. https://sb.co

10. https://lifescienceangels.com/

Appendix

FUNDING TRENDS IN LIFE SCIENCES: KEY RESOURCES

Reports:

Deloitte 2019 US and Global Life Sciences Outlook & Infographic

McKinsey & Co Building Bridges to Innovation, China Pharma Industry

PitchBook 2019 Venture Capital Outlook

PwC / CB Insights MoneyTreeTM Report, Q1 2019- US and global VC funding and deal activity

Silicon Valley Bank Trends in Healthcare Investments & Exits 2019

Timmerman Report-Family Offices That Invest in Biotech Startups

Vantage 2019 Pharma Biotech Preview

Wilson Sonsini Goodrich & Rosati Entrepreneurs Report-private company funding trends

Articles:

Meet the Family Offices that Invest Directly in Biotech, Medtech and Healthcare IT Startups

Navigating the Life Sciences Funding Landscape

Reproduced by kind permission of Judy Robinett, author of *Crack the Funding Code: How Investors Think and What They Need to Hear to Fund Your Startup*

For more information, visit: www.judyrobinett.com; Twitter: @judyrobinett

Acknowledgements

I am extremely grateful to everyone interviewed in this book for their time, their words of wisdom, and their pioneering spirit. I would like to thank everyone that I have quoted, as well as everyone I've ever interviewed for *Thrive Global and Authority Magazine*. This book would not have been possible without you.

Thank you Matt Stone, Michelle Weidenbenner, Sloane Ketchum, Graham Southorn, Yitzi Weiner, Jeff Rieske, Robert Khoury, Jeff Theefs and Debbie Lum for helping me create *The Art of Healthcare Innovation*. I could not have done it without you.

And finally, I would like to thank everyone who has read my interviews, reached out, shared the book, or in any way engaged in conversation.

This book is for you.

About the Author

Christina D. Warner is a healthcare innovator, marketing strategist, and global connector. Christina joined a top Fortune 100 in 2018, and plays a critical role in tactical marketing with disease states such as neurology, multiple sclerosis, gastroenterology, pulmonary and bleeding disorders. Prior to the Fortune 100 company, Christina joined Northwestern Feinberg

School of Medicine and worked in partnership with the Michael J. Fox Foundation on clinical trial initiatives for Parkinson's disease. Christina also worked in an international trading firm, splitting her time equally between Taiwan and China.

Christina is a regular columnist for Arianna Huffington's *Thrive Global* and is known for her thought pieces on the intersection of cutting-edge health-care, marketing innovation and executive interviews. Christina has been quoted in *Forbes*, *US News & World Report*, and *Ivy Exec*, among others. Her articles have appeared in *Apple News*, *Buzzfeed*, and *Authority Magazine*.

Christina received her MBA at The Fuqua School of Business, Duke University, where she earned a concentration on healthcare sector management (HSM).

Twitter: @ChristinDWarner
To keep in touch: christinadwarner.com

Will You Review On Amazon?
Thank you for reading my book!

(Credit: Canva)

I would love to hear from you.
Leave me a REVIEW on Amazon
and let me know what you thought, what you liked,
and what inspired you!

Go forth, and change the world!

—Christina D. Warner

CPSIA information can be obtained
at www.ICGtesting.com
Printed in the USA
FFHW020818111019
55483551-61291FF